MONOLOGUES
for
YOUNG ACTORS

Lorraine Cohen

AVON BOOKS
An Imprint of HarperCollinsPublishers

Permissions, constituting a continuation of the copyright page, are listed on pages iii through vi.

AVON BOOKS
An Imprint of HarperCollinsPublishers
10 East 53rd Street
New York, New York 10022-5299

Copyright © 1994 by Lorraine Cohen
Library of Congress Catalog Card Number: 94-94067
ISBN: 0-380-76187-4
www.avonbooks.com

First Avon Books printing: August 1994

Avon Trademark Reg. U.S. Pat. Off. and in Other Countries, Marca Registrada, Hecho en U.S.A.
HarperCollins® is a trademark of HarperCollins Publishers Inc.

Printed in the U.S.A.

20

ACKNOWLEDGMENTS

ACKNOWLEDGMENTS V

CONTENTS

MONOLOGUES FOR YOUNG WOMEN

MONOLOGUES FOR YOUNG WOMEN

HAPPY BIRTHDAY, WANDA JUNE

Kurt Vonnegut, Jr.

This a satirical play based loosely on Homer's *Odyssey* and Ernest Hemingway. It is introduced by Penelope, one of the characters, as a "simple-minded play about men who enjoy killing and those who don't." It takes place in a room with stuffed animal heads mounted all over the walls. Apparently, someone has ordered a birthday cake but never picked it up. One of the characters in the play has bought it—and brought it home. In typical Vonnegut humor, the girl, Wanda June, for whom the cake was purchased, appears once in the play and talks directly to the audience. There is background music and, according to Vonnegut, she is as "cute as Shirley Temple."

●—◆—●

(MUSIC indicates happiness, innocence, and weightlessness. Spotlight comes up on WANDA JUNE, a lisping eight-year-old in a starched party dress.)

WANDA JUNE.
    Hello. I am Wanda June. Today was going to be my birthday, but I was hit by an ice-cream truck

before I could have my party. I am dead now. I am in Heaven. That is why my parents did not pick up the cake at the bakery. I am not mad at the ice-cream truck driver, even though he was drunk when he hit me. It didn't hurt much. It wasn't even as bad as the sting of a bumblebee. I am really *happy* here! It's so much fun. I am glad the driver was drunk. If he hadn't been, I might not have got to Heaven for years and years and years. I would have had to go to high school first, and then beauty college. I would have had to get married and have babies and everything. Now I can just play and play and play. Any time I want any pink cotton candy I can have some. Everybody up here is happy—the animals and the dead soldiers and people who went to the electric chair and everything. They're all glad for whatever sent them here. Nobody is mad. We're all too busy playing shuffleboard. So if you think of killing somebody, don't worry about it. Just go ahead and do it. Whoever you do it to should kiss you for doing it. The soldiers up here just love the shrapnel and the tanks and the bayonets and the dum dums that let them play shuffle-board all the time—and drink beer.

(Spotlight begins to dim and carnival music on a steam calliope begins to intrude, until, at the end of the speech, WANDA JUNE is drowned out and the stage is black)

We have merry-go-rounds that don't cost any-thing to ride on. We have Ferris wheels. We have Little League and girls' basketball. There's a drum and bugle corps anybody can join. For people who like golf, there is a par-three golf course and a driving range, with never any waiting. If you just want to sit and loaf, why that's all right, too. Gourmet specialities are cooked to your order and served at any time of night or day. . . .

ALICE IN WONDERLAND

Adapted by
Eva Le Gallienne and Florida Friebus

This adaptation of Lewis Carroll's work was first performed in 1947. It is a well-known fantasy about a curious young girl transported to a world where magical things happen. The following monologue opens the play with Alice curled up in an armchair at home and talking to the kitten she is holding.

•◆•

ALICE.
Oh, you wicked, wicked little thing! Really, Dinah ought to have taught you better manners! Now, don't interrupt me! I'm going to tell you all your faults. Number one: you squeaked twice while Dinah was washing your face this morning. Now you can't deny it, Kitty; I heard you. Number two: you pulled Snowdrop away by the tail just as I had put down the saucer of milk before her. Now for number three: you unwound every bit of worsted while I wasn't looking! That's three faults, Kitty, and you've not been punished for any of them yet. You know I'm saving up all your punishments for Wednesday week. Suppose they had saved up all my punishments! What *would* they

do at the end of a year? I should be sent to prison, I suppose, when the day came. Kitty, can you play chess? Now don't smile, my dear, I'm asking it seriously. Because, when we were playing just now, you watched just as if you understood it; and when I said "Check!" you purred! Well, it *was* a nice check, Kitty, and really I might have won, if it hadn't been for that nasty Knight that came wriggling down among my pieces. Kitty dear, let's pretend that you're the Red Queen! Do you know, I think if you sat up and folded your arms, you'd look exactly like her. Now do try, there's a dear! You're not folding your arms properly. I'll just hold you up to the looking glass and you can see how sulky you are! (*She does so.*) And if you're not good directly, I'll put you through into Looking-glass House. How would you like *that?* Now, if you'll only attend, Kitty, I'll tell you all my ideas about Looking-glass House. First, there's the room you can see through the glass . . . that's just the same as our drawing-room, only the things go the other way. Oh, Kitty, how nice it would be if we could only get through into Looking-glass House! I'm sure it's got, oh, such beautiful things in it! Let's pretend there's a way of getting through into it somehow, Kitty. (*She rises and climbs from the arm of the chair to the mantel.*) Let's pretend the glass has got all soft like gauze, so that we can get through. Why, it's turning into a sort of mist now, I declare. It'll be easy enough to get through . . . (ALICE *finds that the glass is indeed like a bright, silvery mist, and she goes through it at once, as LIGHTS dim . . . emerging, presently, on the other side, into the Looking-glass room, LIGHTS UP.*) Oh, what fun it'll be when they see me through the glass in here, and can't get at me! (*She discovers a book lying near her on the mantel, and sits down on the mantelpiece to read it.*) It's all in some language I don't know! Why, it's a Looking-glass book, of course! And if I hold it up to the glass, the words will all go the right way again. (*She holds the book up to the glass reading, as if from its reflection . . .*)

JABBERWOCKY

'Twas brillig, and the slithy toves
Did gyre and gimble in the wabe:
All mimsy were the borogoves,
And the mome raths outgrabe.

"Beware the Jabberwock, my son!
The jaws that bite, the claws that catch!
Beware the Jubjub bird, and shun
The frumious Bandersnatch!"

He took his vorpal sword in hand;
Long time the manxome foe he sought . . .
So rested he by the Tumtum tree,
And stood awhile in thought.

And as in uffish thought he stood,
The Jabberwock, with eyes of flame,
Came whiffling through the tulgey wood,
And burbled as it came!

One, two! One, two! And through and through
The vorpal blade went snickersnack!
He left it dead, and with its head
He went galumphing back.

"And hast thou slain the Jabberwock?
Come to my arms, my beamish boy!
O frabjous day! Callooh! Callay!"
He chortled in his joy.

'Twas brillig, and the slithy toves
Did gyre and gimble in the wabe;
All mimsy were the borogoves,
And the mome raths outgrabe.

It seems very pretty, but it's *rather* hard to understand! Somehow it seems to fill my head with
ideas ... only I don't exactly know what they
are! However, *somebody* killed *something:* that's
clear, at any rate ...

THE DIARY OF ANNE FRANK

Frances Goodrich and Albert Hackett

This play is adapted from the diary kept by Anne
Frank as she and her family hid from the Nazis
in Amsterdam during World War II. In 1942 eight
Jews—the Franks, the Van Daans and Dr. Dussel,
a dentist—sought asylum in the attic of a warehouse belonging to Mr. Frank's firm. These hunted
people lived together for two years, depending on
four former employees of Mr. Frank for food and
necessities. Anne began her diary at the age of 13,
and has given the world a tender, beautiful docu-
ment about a girl growing up and the human spirit
under terrible adversity. The attic hiding place was
discovered in 1944 and its inhabitants were sent to
concentration camps. In the next few months, they
all died except for Otto Frank, who was freed in
1945 by the Russians. When Amsterdam was lib-
erated, he returned and was given the diary that
Miep, one of their benefactors during their hiding,
had saved.

The following monologue is from a scene near
the very end of the play. Peter Van Daan, a quiet and unhappy seventeen-year-old has just rushed
into his little room in despair. Anne, displaying
developing maturity, is trying to console him.

It is the last time they are together for the scene immediately precedes the entrance of the Nazis. The asterisks indicate Peter's short responses.

• ◆ •

ANNE.

Look, Peter, the sky. (*She looks up through skylight.*) What a lovely, lovely day! Aren't the clouds beautiful? You know what I do when it seems as if I couldn't stand being cooped up for one more minute? I *think* myself out. I think myself on a walk in the park where I used to go with Pim. Where the jonquils and the crocus and the violets grow down the slopes. You know the most wonderful thing about *thinking* yourself out? You can have it any way you like. You can have roses and violets and chrysanthemums all blooming at the same time . . . it's funny . . . I used to take it all for granted . . . and now I've gone crazy about everything to do with nature. Haven't you?

(*Softly.*) I wish you had a religion, Peter.

*   *   *

Oh, I don't mean you have to be Orthodox . . . or believe in heaven and hell and purgatory and things. . . . I just mean some religion . . . it doesn't matter what. Just to believe in something! When I think of all that's out there. . . . the trees . . . and flowers . . . and seagulls . . . When I think of the dearness of you, Peter . . . and the goodness of the people we know . . . Mr. Kraler, Miep, Dirk, the vegetable man, all risking their lives for us every day. . . . When I think of these good things,

I'm not afraid any more. . . . I find myself, and
God, and I. . . .

* * *

We're not the only people that've had to suffer. There've always been people that've had
to . . . sometimes one race . . . sometimes another . . . and yet. . . .

* * *

I know it's terrible, trying to have any faith . . .
when people are doing such horrible . . . but you
know what I sometimes think? I think the world
may be going through a phase, the way I was
with Mother, It'll pass, maybe not for hundreds of
years, but some day. . . . I still believe, in spite of
everything, that people are really good at heart.

* * *

Peter, if you'd only look at it as part of a great
pattern . . . that we're just a little minute in life . . .
(*She breaks off.*) Listen to us, going at each other like
a couple of stupid grownups! Look at the sky now,
Isn't it lovely? (*She holds out her hand to him.*)

STREET SCENE

Elmer Rice

This play takes place during two days of a hot summer in the 1920s. All the scenes occur in front of a walk-up apartment building, which plays a central role to the play. It is from this building that characters of different ethnic backgrounds look out the windows, sit on the front stoop, enter and depart, or just walk by. A young Jewish boy named Sam has fallen in love with Rose, a neighbor from a troubled Irish family. The following monologue by Rose is taken from a scene between the young people. Deletions of Sam's short protest lines are marked by asterisks.

• ◆ •

ROSE.
 Well, I haven't really had any time to do much thinking. But I really think the best thing I could do, would be to get out of New York. You know, like we were saying, this morning—how things might be different, if you only had a chance to breathe and spread out a little. Only when I said it, I never dreamt it would be this way.

13

*   *   *

I like you so much, Sam. I like you better than anybody I know.

*   *   *

It would be so nice to be with you. You're different from anybody I know. But I'm just wondering how it would work out.

*   *   *

There's lots of things to be considered. Suppose something was to happen—well, suppose I was to have a baby, say. That sometimes happens, even when you don't want it to. What would we do, then? We'd be tied down then, for life, just like all the other people around here. They all start out loving each other and thinking that everything is going to be fine—and before you know it, they find out they haven't got anything and they wish they could do it all over again—only it's too late.

*   *   *

It's what you said just now—about people belonging to each other. I don't think people ought to belong to anybody but themselves. I was thinking, that if my mother had really belonged to herself, and that if my father had really belonged to himself, it never would have happened. It was only because they were always depending on somebody else, for what they ought to have had inside themselves. Do you see what I mean, Sam? That's why I don't want to belong to anybody, and why I don't want anybody to belong to me.

* * *

I want love more than anything else in the world. But loving and belonging aren't the same thing. [*Putting her arms about him*]: Sam dear, listen. If we say good-bye, now, it doesn't mean that it has to be forever. Maybe some day, when we're older and wiser, things will be different. Don't look as if it was the end of the world, Sam!

* * *

It isn't, Sam! If you'd only believe in yourself, a little more, things wouldn't look nearly so bad. Because once you're sure of yourself, the things that happen to you, aren't so important. The way I look at it, it's not what you do that matters so much; it's what you are. [*Warmly*]: I'm so fond of you, Sam. And I've got such a lot of confidence in you. [*Impulsively*]: Give me a nice kiss!

ONE SUNDAY AFTERNOON

James Hagan

This lovely, if somewhat sentimental play, written in 1930, is about young love in a small Midwestern town. Amy, a romantic young girl, has a crush on the town bully. One exclamation by her friend is deleted and marked by asterisks.

◆

AMY.

I don't know. Maybe it was love, I don't know, but—

* * *

Well, when I was very young—of course, that's a long time ago, you understand—[VIRGINA *nods*.] It was in school. There was a boy. I don't know— he never looked at me and I never—[*She looks at* VIRGINIA *wistfully*.] Virginia, did you ever have a feeling in your heart—Something that you feel is going to happen and it doesn't—that's the way my heart was—[*She touches her heart*.] It wasn't love, I know that—[*Pause*.] He never even noticed me. I could have been a stick-in-the-mud as far

16

as he was concerned. Virginia, this boy always seemed lonely somehow. Everybody had it in for him, even the teachers—they called him bully— but I know he wasn't. I saw him do a lot of good things—when the big boys picked on the smaller ones, he helped the little fellows out. I know he had a lot of good in him—good, that nobody else could see—that's why my heart—

SAINT JOAN

George Bernard Shaw

The story of Joan of Arc, the illiterate teenage girl who hears voices and leads soldiers into battle, is legendary. But this play does not romanticize her or present her only as a courageous visionary. Instead, the play shows Joan as a girl who wants to lead a man's life, a girl too young to understand tact and, yet, old enough to be shrewd. The author portrays Joan's enemies not as villains but as men convinced that they are doing the right thing.

The setting of the play is fifteenth-century France. The following monologue takes place on May 30, 1431, at Rouen in the great stone hall of the castle. The hall has been arranged for a trial-at-law, rather than a trial-by-jury. Joan, chained by the ankles, has just been told by her inquisitors that instead of being burned at the stake for heresy, she will be imprisoned for life.

•◆•

JOAN.

Yes: they told me you were fools [*the word gives great offence*], and that I was not to listen to your fine words nor trust to your charity. You promised me my life; but you lied [*indignant exclama-tions*]. You think that life is nothing but not being stone dead. It is not the bread and water I fear: I can live on bread: when have I asked for more? It is no hardship to drink water if the water be clean. Bread has no sorrow for me, and water no affliction. But to shut me from the light of the sky and the sight of the fields and flowers; to chain my feet so that I can never again ride with the soldiers nor climb the hills; to make me breathe foul damp darkness, and keep from me everything that brings me back to the love of God when your wickedness and foolishness tempt me to hate Him: all this is worse than the furnace in the Bible that was heated seven times. I could do without my warhorse; I could drag about in a skirt; I could let the banners and the trumpets and the knights and soldiers pass me and leave me behind as they leave the other women, if only I could still hear the wind in the trees, the larks in the sunshine, the young lambs crying through the healthy frost, and the blessed blessed church bells that send my angel voices floating to me on the wind. But without these things I cannot live; and by your wanting to take them away from me, or from any human creature, I know that your counsel is of the devil, and that mine is of God.

THE EFFECT OF GAMMA RAYS ON MAN-IN-THE-MOON MARIGOLDS

Paul Zindel

This touching play—which the author, in an introduction, infers is somewhat autobiographical—is essentially about a courageous, pathetic, and outrageous woman trying to keep her family and life afloat. Her family consists of two daughters who are as different from each other as possible. Ruth is a blatant flirt, rebellious, and argumentative. Tillie is the student, fascinated by science and also sensitive to her eccentric mother's feelings. The following monologue opens the play, beginning with a musical recording in the dark.

•◆•

(The lights go down slowly as music creeps in—a theme for lost children, the near misbegotten.
From the blackness TILLIE'S VOICE *speaks against the music.)*

TILLIE'S VOICE.
He told me to look at my hand, for a part of it came from a star that exploded too long ago to imagine. This part of me was formed from a tongue of fire that screamed through the heav-

ens until there was our sun. And this part of
me—this tiny part of me—was on the sun when
it itself exploded and whirled in a great storm
until the planets came to be.

(Lights start in.)

And this small part of me was then a whisper of
the earth. When there was life, perhaps this part
of me got lost in a fern that was crushed and cov-
ered until it was coal. And then it was a diamond
millions of years later—it must have been a diamond as beautiful as the star from which it had
first come.

Taking over from recorded voice.

Or perhaps this part of me became lost in a terrible beast, or became part of a huge bird that flew
above the primeval swamps.

And he said this thing was so small—this part of
me was so small it couldn't be seen—but it was
there from the beginning of the world.

And he called this bit of me an atom. And when
he wrote the word, I fell in love with it.
Atom.
Atom.
What a beautiful word.

THE EFFECT OF GAMMA RAYS ON MAN-IN-THE-MOON MARIGOLDS

Paul Zindel

This second monologue from the play is delivered as a speech at a high school science fair by one of the contestants, who apparently is overly satisfied about herself and her accomplishment with a rather ludicrous experiment. This is in contrast to the serious science project presented by Tillie. For more background on this play, see the previous introduction on page 20.

•—◆—•

JANICE.

The Past: I got the cat from the A.S.P.C.A. immediately after it had been killed by a high-altitude pressure system. That explains why some of the rib bones are missing, because that method sucks the air out of the animal's lungs and ruptures all cavities. They say it prevents cruelty to animals but I think it's horrible.

(She laughs.)

Then I boiled the cat in a sodium hydroxide solution until most of the skin pulled right off, but I had to scrape some of the grizzle off the joints with a knife. You have no idea how difficult it is to get right down to the bones.

(A little gong sounds.)

I have to go on to *The Present*, now—but I did want to tell you how long it took me to put the thing together. I mean, as it is now, it's extremely useful for students of anatomy, even with the missing rib bones, and it can be used to show basic anatomical aspects of many, many animals that are in the same family as felines. I suppose that's about the only present uses I can think for it, but it is nice to remember as an accomplishment, and it looks good on college applications to show you did something else in school besides dating.

(She laughs, and a second gong sounds.)

The Future: The only future plans I have for Tabby—my little brother asked the A.S.P.C.A. what its name was when he went to pick it up and they said it was called Tabby, but I think they were kidding him—

(She laughs again.)

I mean as far as future plans, I'm going to donate it to the science department, of course, and next year, if there's another Science Fair perhaps I'll do the same thing with a dog.

(A third gong sounds.)

Thank you very much for your attention, and I hope I win!

ANTIGONE

Jean Anouilh

This version of the Greek classic was first produced in Paris in 1944. The old questions of conscience versus the law and the conflict between idealism and pragmatism have been with us since societies were first formed. They became especially pertinent during World War II when Jean Anouilh adapted the play. He did not fully modernize it, however, as the play still takes place in ancient Greece. Anouilh also retained many of the conventions of Greek tragedy, such as the use of the chorus.

Antigone's uncle, the king of Thebes, has ordered that the body of her brother, Polynices, be left to rot because of his treachery against the crown. The King orders punishment of death for anyone attempting to give Polynices a true burial. But Antigone defies the king and his order. In the following scene with her sister, Ismene, Antigone has not made it known that she has already done the deed. Ismene's lines are deleted and marked by asterisks.

◆

ANTIGONE.

But I am not the king; and I don't have ~~~set~~ people examples. Little Antigone gets a notion in her head—the nasty brat, the willful, wicked girl; and they put her in a corner all day, or they lock her up in the cellar. And she deserves it. She shouldn't have disobeyed!

*   *   *

I don't want to be right!

*   *   *

Understand! The first word I ever heard out of any of you was that word "understand." Why didn't I "understand" that I must not play with water—cold, black, beautiful flowing water—because I'd spill it on the palace tiles. Or with earth, because earth dirties a little girl's frock. Why didn't I "understand" that nice children don't eat out of every dish at once; or give everything in their pockets to beggars; or run in the wind so fast that they fall down; or ask for a drink when they're perspiring; or want to go swimming when it's either too early or too late, merely because they happen to feel like swimming. Understand! I don't want to understand. There'll be time enough to understand when I'm old. . . . If I ever *am* old. But not now.

ANTIGONE

Jean Anouilh

Ismene, the beautiful sister of Antigone, represents the viewpoint opposite Antigone's. She is the realist and is not willing to die for a cause. In this monologue, she tries to talk Antigone out of defying the king, not knowing that Antigone has already buried her brother. For more about this provocative play, see the previous introduction on page 24.

●◆●

ISMENE.
His mob will come running, howling as it runs. A thousand arms will seize our arms. A thousand breaths will breathe into our faces. Like one single pair of eyes, a thousand eyes will stare at us. We'll be driven in a tumbrel through their hatred, through the smell of them and their cruel, roaring laughter. We'll be dragged to the scaffold for torture, surrounded by guards with their idiot faces all bloated, their animal hands clean-washed for the sacrifice, their beefy eyes squinting as they stare at us. And we'll know that no shrieking and no begging will make them understand that we want to live, for they are

like slaves who do exactly as they've been told, without caring about right or wrong. And we shall suffer, we shall feel pain rising in us until it becomes so unbearable that we *know* it must stop. But it won't stop; it will go on rising and rising, like a screaming voice. Oh, I can't, I can't, Antigone!

BALM IN GILEAD

Lanford Wilson

In this play, Darlene is described as an attractive young woman about twenty years old. She speaks with a Midwestern twang and is not very intelligent. In this monologue, she talks to Ann, a prostitute who, along with other misfits, hangs out at this all-night coffee shop. Ann's lines are deleted and marked by asterisks. For more on this play, see page 184.

• ◆ •

DARLENE.
  [*pause*]. I know one thing: I sure feel like you do about marriage. I mean, I just don't know. Like you said. I know this guy I used to go with—when I first got a room of my own, up on Armitage Street? Do you know that part of Chicago?

*   *   *

Oh. Well, most of the streets run either east and west or up and down, you know—one or the other. But some of them kinna cut across all the

28

others—Armitage Street does, and some of the other real nice ones. Fullerton Street does.

I don't know if it's important, but Fullerton Street does not. In other words, DARLENE *rather prefers the vivid to the accurate.*

And they're wider, you know, with big trees and all, and there are all of these big old lovely apartment buildings, very well taken care of, with little lawns out front and flower boxes in the windows and all. You know what I mean? And the rents, compared to what they try to sock you with here. The rents are practically nothing—even in this neighborhood. [*Pause.*] My apartment was two flights up, in the front. It was so cute, you'd have loved it. They had it all done over when I moved in. I had three rooms. And let's see—there was just a lovely big living room that looked out onto Armitage Street and a real cute little kitchen and then the bedroom—that looked out onto a garden in the back and on the other side of the garden was Grant Park— or some park, I never did know the name it had. But there were kids that I just loved playing out in this park all the time. And then I had this little bathroom, a private bath. I had—it was funny— I had a collection—you know practically everybody collects something. . . .

*   *   *

[*laughs*]. No, not like that! I collected towels, if you must know. You know, from all the big hotels—Of course, I didn't get very many of them myself, but friends of mine, every time they went anywhere always brought me back a big bath towel or hand towel or face towel with some new name across it. I'll swear, I never bought one towel in all the time I lived there! It was funny, too, it looked real great in a regular bathroom like that; these hotel names. Everyone just loved it. My favorite one was—from this—oh, this real elegant hotel—what was it's— I don't even remember the name any more I had so many of them. Anyway, the apartment, in that neighborhood and all, cost me practically nothing compared to what they want for a place not half as good in New York. And I lived there, and this guy I was going with, you know, that asked me to marry him? He lived across the hall. He moved into the apartment next to mine. Really, Ann, you should have seen him. He was slow, everything he did, and quiet; he hardly ever talked at all. You had to just pump him to get him to say the time of day. And he had white hair—nearly white; they used to call him Cotton—he told me— when he was in Alabama. That's where he's from. He was living in the apartment next to mine and we were always together, and there just wasn't any difference between his place and mine. We should have only been paying for one rent. Half of his stuff was in my place and half vice versa. He used to get so pissed off when I'd wash things out and hang them up in his bathroom or in the kitchen and all. You know, over the fire there. But we were always together—and we finally decided to get married—we both did. And all our friends were buying rice and digging out their old shoes. Cotton—he worked in a television fac-tory, RCA, I believe, but I couldn't be sure. That's why I started thinking about him when you said this Sam had electrical parts all over the apart-

ment. Old Cotton had, I'll swear, the funniest
temperament I ever saw. If he got mad—[*Almost
as though mad.*]—he wouldn't argue or anything
like that, he'd just walk around like nothing was
wrong only never say one word. Sometimes for
two or three days. And that used to get me so
mad I couldn't stand it. Have you ever known
anyone who did that?

*   *   *

Just wouldn't talk at all, I mean. Not say one
word for days.

*   *   *

It used to just burn me up. And he knew it did,
is what made it so bad. I'd just be so mad I
could spit. And I'd say something like: *what's
wrong, Cotton?* And just as easy as you please
he'd reach over and light a cigarette and look out
the window or something. Turn on the radio. I
just wish I had the control to be like that because
it is the most maddening thing you can possibly do to someone when they're trying to argue
with you. I could do it for about five minutes,
then I'd blow my stack. Oh, I used to get so
damn mad at him. *Agh!* [*Pause.*] Course I make
it sound worse than it was, cause he didn't act
like that very often. Fortunately. But you never
knew what was going to provoke him, I swear.
It was just that we saw each other every hour of
every day—you just couldn't get us apart. And
when we decided to get married all our friends
were so excited—of course, they'd been expecting it probably. But we were so crazy you'd nev-

er know what we were going to do. I know he used to set the TV so it pointed into the mirror, because there wasn't a plug-in by the bed and we'd lay there in bed and look at the mirror that had the TV reflected in it. Only everything was backwards. Writing was backwards. [*She laughs.*] Only, you know, even backwards, it was a better picture, it was clearer than if you was just looking straight at it.

A RAISIN IN THE SUN

Lorraine Hansberry

This play, written in 1959, is set in Chicago's Southside "sometime between World War II and the Present." The title is taken from a poem by Langston Hughes, and the play itself is about a black family struggling to better itself in a hostile world. The following monologue is delivered by Beneatha, the headstrong and ambitious grandaughter. She is speaking to a young African student who is obviously interested in her. His few lines during this passage are deleted and marked by asterisks.

•◆•

BENEATHA.
Me? . . . Me? . . . Me, I'm nothing . . . Me. When I was very small . . . we used to take our sleds out in the wintertime and the only hills we had were the ice-covered stone steps of some houses down the street. And we used to fill them in with snow and make them smooth and slide down them all day . . . and it was very dangerous you know . . . far too steep . . . and sure enough one day a kid named Rufus came down too fast and hit the sidewalk . . . and we saw his face just split

open right there in front of us . . . And I remember standing there looking at his bloody open face thinking that was the end of Rufus. But the ambulance came and they took him to the hospital and they fixed the broken bones and they sewed it all up . . . and the next time I saw Rufus he just had a little line down the middle of his face . . . I never got over that . . .

*   *   *

That that was what one person could do for another, fix him up—sew up the problem, make him all right again. That was the most marvelous thing in the world . . . I wanted to do that. I always thought it was the one concrete thing in the world that a human being could do. Fix up the sick, you know—and make them whole again. This was truly being God . . .

*   *   *

No—I wanted to cure. It used to be so important to me. I wanted to cure. It used to matter. I used to care. I mean about people and how their bodies hurt . . .

BUTTERFLIES ARE FREE

Leonard Gershe

◆

Jill is nineteen and has just come in for coffee to meet her neighbor, Don. In this scene, they are getting to know each other. Don's lines have been deleted and marked by asterisks as Jill talks about an early, failed marriage. She hasn't, as yet, caught on to his blindness. For more on this play, see page 161.

JILL.

No, I will talk about him. (*Crosses above coffee table.*) Once in a while it's good for you to do something you don't want to do. It cleanses the insides. He was terribly sweet and groovy-looking, but kind of adolescent, you know what I mean? (*Flicks ash into ashtray.*) Girls mature faster than boys. Boys are neater, but girls mature faster. (*Sits in director's chair.*) When we met it was like fireworks. I don't know if I'm saying it right, but it was a marvelous kind of passion that made every day like the Fourth of July. Anyway, the next thing I knew we were standing in front of a justice of the peace getting married.

35

* * *

Two or three weeks, but I mean there we were getting *married!* (*Sits back in chair, feet on stool.*) I hadn't even finished high school and I had two exams the next day and they were on my mind, too. (*Rises, crosses through kitchen to* D. L. *post.*) I heard the justice of the peace saying, "Do you, *Jack*, take Jill to be your lawfully wedded wife?" Can you imagine going through life as Jack and Jill? And then I heard "Till death do you part" and, suddenly, it wasn't a wedding ceremony. It was a funeral service.

* * *

(*Crosses below to* R. *bench.*) You know that wedding ceremony is very morbid when you think about it. I hate anything morbid and there I was being buried alive . . . under Jack Benson. I wanted to run screaming out into the night!

* * *

(*Turns, crosses* D.R. *post.*) I couldn't. It was ten o'clock in the morning. I mean you can't go screaming out into ten o'clock in the morning . . . so I passed out. If only I'd fainted before I said "I do."

* * *

(*Crosses to coffee table, picks up ashtray.*) I did try— believe me. I tried for six days, but I knew it was no good.

* * *

(*Crosses to ladder, climbs to second or third step.*) I don't know. . . . Well, I think just because you love someone that doesn't necessarily mean that you want to spend the rest of your life with him. But Jack loved me. I mean he really, really loved me and I hurt him and that's what I can't stand. I just never want to hurt anybody. (*Off ladder through kitchen to* U. *end of table*.) I mean marriage is a commitment, isn't it? I just can't be committed or involved. Can you understand?

LITTLE MURDERS

Jules Feiffer

This rather bizarre comedy begins with Patsy, the All-American girl, bringing home her new boyfriend, Alfred. She lives with her mother, father, and brother in an apartment in a big city, but there the conventional family play ends. An early clue comes from the sounds in the background—not the usual city noises of traffic but sporadic gunfire and the sound of a toilet flushing. The following monologue takes place right after the young couple's unusual wedding ceremony. Patsy is trying to argue with her new husband who won't argue back and whom she has accused of lacking feelings. Two short comments by Alfred are deleted and marked by asterisks. Patsy is shot through the window right after this scene, and the play ends with a very satirical twist.

•◆•

PATSY.

Honey, I don't want to hurt you. I want to change you. I want to save you. I want to make you see that there is some value in life, that there is some beauty, some tenderness, some things

worth reacting to. Some things *worth* feeling—
(*Snaps fingers in front of his eyes.* Come back here!
I swear, Alfred, *nobody* is going to kill you. But
you've got to take some *chances* sometime! What
do you want out of life? Just *survival?*

*   *   *

It's not enough! It's not, not, not enough! I'm not
going to have a surviving marriage, I'm going to
have a flourishing marriage! I'm a *woman!* Or,
by Jesus, it's about time I became one. I want
a family! Oh, Christ, Alfred, this is my wedding
day—(*Pause. Regains composure.*) I want—I want
to be married to a big, strong, protective, vital,
virile, self-assured man. Who I can protect and
take care of. Alfred, honey, you're the first man
I've ever gone to bed with where I didn't feel *he*
was a lot more likely to get pregnant than I was.
(*Desperate.*) You owe me something! I've invested
everything I believe in you. You've *got* to let
me mold you. *Please* let me mold you. (*Regains
control.*) You've got me begging. You're got me
whining, begging and crying. I've never behaved
like this in my life. Will you look at this? (*Holds
out finger.*) That's a tear. I never cried in my life.

*   *   *

You never cried because you were too terrified of
everything to let yourself *feel!* You'd have to learn
crying from a manual! Chop onions! I never cried
because I was too tough—but I felt *everything.*
Every slight, every pressure, every vague com-
petition—but I *fought.* And I *won!* There hasn't
been a battle since I was five that I haven't won!

And the people I fought were happy that I won! *Happy!* After a while. Alfred, do you have any idea how many people in this town *worship* me? Maybe that's the attraction—you don't worship me. (*Shakes head.*) Maybe I'd lose all respect for you if you did all the things I want you to do. (*Thinks on it.*) Alfred, *you've got* to change! (*Regains calm.*) Listen. (*Pause.*) I'm not saying I'm better or stronger than you are. It's just that we—you and I—have different temperaments. (*Explodes.*) *And my temperament is better and stronger than yours!* (*Frantic.*) You're a *wall!* (*Circles him.*) You don't fight! You hardly ever listen! Dear God, will somebody please explain to me why I think you're so beautiful. (*PHONE rings. She picks it up. Amplified BREATHING.*) *Leave me alone! What do you want out of me? Will you please leave me alone?*

SABRINA FAIR

Samuel Taylor

Sabrina is the vivacious daughter of the chauffeur for a wealthy family on the North Shore of Long Island. She has just returned home after three years in Paris and is described by one character as an "earnest scholarly little mouse" when she graduated from college and before she left for France. Sabrina is now, at this homecoming, described as chic and apparently in "love with the world." The part was played by the famous Margaret Sullavan in New York City in 1953 with co–stars Cathleen Nesbitt and Joseph Cotton.

The following scene takes place just as Sabrina enters the room. Maude, her father's employer, doesn't immediately recognize her but then gives her a warm welcome. Some of Maude's short lines, as well as lines by other characters, are deleted and marked by asterisks as Sabrina chatters happily.

•◆•

SABRINA.
    Oh, I was hoping you wouldn't recognize me! Have I changed? Have I really changed? (*She backs up a bit, hanging on to* MAUDE'S *hands*) I'm

41

so glad to see you! David, you didn't recognize
me, either did you? (*He shakes his head, fascinated*)
Ah! Then I have changed, haven't I? I don't mean
just the clothes, that's easy. But me! Myself! Do
I seem very different? Here! Now! Without the
hat! (*And she tears off the smart, ridiculous little hat,
and shakes out her hair*) Now!

*   *   *

How wonderful! I wanted to hear you say that.
Is that vain of me? I don't mean it to sound vain.
But I thought it would be such fun to hear you
say it. Because I *feel* so different! It was the first
thing I thought of when I woke up this morning, as the ship was coming up the bay. And
then later, lying in my berth, having breakfast—
my last breakfast of that good French bread and
that horrible coffee that I love so—I thought: (*She
closes her eyes and tells her dream, with a soft smile*)
what fun it will be . . . they'll all be in the garden, in the walled garden off the terrace . . . and
I'll come running in to them to say hello. And
they'll say: "Sabrina? Is it Sabrina? Why, Sabrina,
we didn't recognize you!" (*She opens her eyes and
grins*) And that's the way it happened! Ah! I
think if you had just said, "Oh, hello, Sabrina,
how are you?" I'd have died. (*She whirls on* JULIA)
You don't remember me, but I remember you. I
used to peek around corners at you.

*   *   *

You're famous in Paris, did you know that? I
kept hearing about you all the time. It seems
as though everybody knows you. And they tell

such wonderful stories about you, in the twenties: about you and Picasso and Gertrude Stein, and the book shop you ran, and the magazine . . . It must be fun to be part of a legend.

*   *   *

Paris was the most exciting place in the world, then, wasn't it?

*   *   *

It still is. (*She turns and yells*) Father? (*Her father has appeared from the garage court*) I wish you could have seen Father at the station. He was completely baffled. There I was, charging across the platform at him, yelling, "Father!," and he kept looking over his shoulder to see who my father was! (*She crosses to him swiftly, smiling at him lovingly*) I finally had to leap at him to make him recognize me, didn't I Father? And the most terrible thing happened! I leaped too hard and knocked him down! Right there in front of all Glen Cove! Father! The most dignified man on Long Island! (*She gives him an affectionate peck on the cheek*) Thank goodness it wasn't a commuters' train.

*   *   *

Oh! (*She looks over to the others anxiously*) Am I being too . . . too . . .

*   *   *

It's just that I'm so excited. (*With rueful humor, softly, to her father*) I'm sorry, Father. I shall keep my place as soon as I know it. But for now, do be an angel and get that thing out of the station wagon for me. You know: the . . . (*She secretly mouths the word "bird" at him, and urges him off*) . . . I want to give it to her now. And be careful of it, please! (*She watches him go, with a fond smile, then turns back to* MAUDE) . . . I brought you something from Paris. Do you mind? It was given me by a beau, and I fell madly in love with it. And then I knew I would have to bring it home to you.

*   *   *

(*With deep affection*) It's something I hope will make you laugh. I wanted to bring it to you because I remembered how you laughed and how I loved so to hear you when I was a little girl.

*   *   *

(*Softly*) Isn't it strange of the English language, and typical, that there is no feminine analogue of "hero worship?"

THE SEA GULL

Anton Chekhov

This lifelike and lovely play by one of the greatest dramatists of modern times made the Moscow Art Theater famous in 1898. The play had been performed a year before and had been a failure then, under the influence of Constantin Stanislavsky, the performances became more subtle and realistic and the play, in turn, became an enormous success.

A group of people are staying at the estate of Peter Sorin. His sister, Madame Arkadina, an aging and flamboyant actress, is visiting with her entourage, which includes Trigorin, her current lover. Nina, a young girl who aspires to be an actress, is very much in love with Trigorin. She is eventually seduced by him, has a child, leaves him, and becomes an actress, albeit second-rate. She returns to the estate briefly and in the following monologue talk's to Trepleff, a young writer who loves her. She had changed and reveals herself no longer innocent, optimistic, or happy.

•◆•

NINA.
Why do you say you kiss the ground I walk on?

I ought to be killed. (*Bends over desk*) I'm so tired. If I could rest . . . rest. I'm a sea gull. No, that's not it. I'm an actress. Well, no matter. . . . (*Hears* ARKADINA *and* TRIGORIN *laughing in the dining room. She listens, runs to the door on the left and peeps through the keyhole*) And he's here too. (*Goes to* TREPLEFF) Well, no matter. He didn't believe in the theatre, all my dreams he'd laugh at, and little by little I quit believing in it myself, and lost heart. And there was the strain of love, jealousy, constant anxiety about my little baby. I got to be small and trashy, and played without thinking. I didn't know what to do with my hands, couldn't stand properly on the stage, couldn't control my voice. You can't imagine the feeling when you are acting and know it's dull. I'm a sea gull. No, that's not it. Do you remember, you shot a sea gull? A man comes by chance, sees it, and out of nothing else to do, destroys it. That's not it . . . (*Puts her hand to her forehead*) What was I . . . I was talking about the stage. Now I'm not like that. I'm a real actress, I act with delight, with rapture, I'm drunk when I'm on the stage, and feel that I am beautiful. And now, ever since I've been here, I've kept walking about, kept walking and thinking, thinking and believing my soul grows stronger every day. Now I know, I understand, Kostya, that in our work . . . acting or writing . . . what matters is not fame, not glory, not what I used to dream about, it's how to endure, to bear my cross, and have faith. I have faith and it all doesn't hurt me so much, and when I think of my calling I'm not afraid of life.

THE SPOON RIVER ANTHOLOGY

Edgar Lee Masters

This beautiful piece does not fit in the conventional mold of a play. Though usually staged and acted by a few actors, it is a collection of poems and songs by many characters. The epitaphs reveal the secret lives of Americans in a small town.

In the following monologue, Flossie Cabanis tells the audience about her painful past.

●—◆—●

FLOSSIE CABANIS.
From Bindle's Opera House in the village
To Broadway is a great step.
But I tried to take it, my ambition fired
When sixteen years of age,
Seeing "East Lynne" played here in the village
By Ralph Barrett, the coming
Romantic actor, who enthralled my soul.
True, I trailed back home, a broken failure,
When Ralph disappeared in New York,
Leaving me alone in the city—
But life broke him also.
In all this place of silence

There are no kindred spirits.
How I wish Duse could stand amid the pathos
Of these quiet fields
And read these words.

THE SPOON RIVER
ANTHOLOGY

Edgar Lee Masters

This is another lovely, confessional poem narrated by Lucinda Matlock. For more background on this play, see page 47.

•◆•

LUCINDA MATLOCK.
   I went to the dances at Chandlerville,
   And played snap-out at Winchester.
   One time we changed partners,
   Driving home in the moonlight of middle June,
   And then I found Davis.
   We were married and lived together for seventy
      years,
   Enjoying, working, raising the twelve children,
   Eight of whom we lost
   Ere I had reached the age of sixty.
   I spun, I wove, I kept the house, I nursed the
      sick,
   I made the garden, and for holiday
   Rambled over the fields where sang the larks,
   And by Spoon River gathering many a shell,
   And many a flower and medicinal weed—

Shouting to the wooded hills, singing to the
   green valleys.
At ninety-six I had lived enough, that is all,
And passed to a sweet repose.
What is this I hear of sorrow and weariness,
Anger, discontent and drooping hopes?
Degenerate sons and daughters,
Life is too strong for you—
It takes life to love life.

IN NEW ENGLAND WINTER

Ed Bullins

In this strong, graphic, and sometimes violent black play, Liz is an eighteen-year-old, exotic-looking woman. In this scene, she is talking to her relatives about her boyfriend, Steve, who is described as a twenty-four-year-old "brooder and thinker." The scene takes place in Liz's kitchen, and there is Count Basie music playing in the background. This is actually two short monologues by Liz with a few intervening lines from other characters deleted and marked by asterisks.

●◆●

(LIZ'S *place.* LIZ, OSCAR *and* CARRIE *sit about the kitchen table. Joe Williams sings "Goin' to Chicago" over the drug store radio. And Count Basie plays through the remainder of the scene.*)

LIZ.
When we was little girls, Carrie and me . . . we didn't even know what snow was . . . when we was down there in Florida. West Palm Beach didn't even have a lick of snow. I remember

51

the mangoes that I fed Carrie . . . and the sapo-
dillas . . . and the kumquats. Someday I'm goin'
back there and just sit in the sun and stick my
feet in the sand and look out into the water.

*   *   *

Steve's lived in snow all his life. All his life. I guess
that's why he's so cold most of the time. A cold,
hard northern black bastard . . . Ha ha . . . he'd be
mad if he heard me call him black, more than
my callin' him bastard . . . I do that all the time.
Don't like that first word none, but he sure likes
me cause I'm black. Said to me . . . "The blacker
the berry . . . the sweeter the juice." Sounded like
some whiteman . . . cause I'm the blackest girl
he's ever been with . . . his mamma didn't want
him to fool round with no real black girls . . .
leastwise that's what he said. Said his mamma
said for him to find a light skinned girl . . . "To
put some color in the family." . . . But I'm black
as sin . . . and that's why he loves me so much.
No danger of me lightenin' up his family none.
(Sighs.) Yeah, he's cold as snow and as brown as
a coconut. Hummp . . . listen to me . . . soundin'
like my auntie. But I love him . . . but he's so wild
and crazy. Wild like only a northern nigger can
be wild. All of it inside, mostly, and cold and
sharp and slick like ice. But I love him cause I
need him.

A MONTH IN THE COUNTRY

Ivan Turgenev

The tranquility of a household of an estate near
Moscow in the early 1840s is disrupted with the
appearance of a new tutor, Beliaev. Although he
is shy and unsophisticated, Beliaev is imaginative
and high-spirited. Natalia is a few years older, married, beautiful, poised, and bored with a current
suitor. She also has fallen in love with Beliaev.
Natalia has even resorted to manipulation, trying
to get rid of her ward, a seventeen-year-old girl
whom she considers a rival. Natalia also has tried
to dismiss Beliaev but is unable to do so. In the following garden scene, she confesses her love to him.
Two attempted interjections by Beliaev are deleted
and marked by asterisks.

●◆●

NATALIA.
The only possible way in which I can hope to
regain your respect—and my own—is to be perfectly frank. Besides, as we shall never see each
other again—this is the last time I shall ever
speak to you. (*Going to him*) She was telling the
truth. I love you.

(*A pause.*)

*   *   *

(*With a strained and deliberate calm*) From the very first day, I loved you; though it was only yesterday that I was fully aware of it.

*   *   *

(*Crossing quickly*) One thing—please understand that it is pride, and pride only, that gives me the courage to tell you this; the farce of pretending revolted me to the marrow—(*Sitting on the seat*) and I have been desperately anxious to wipe from your mind this picture of a tyrannical, cunning creature—anxious that the memory of me which you take away, shall not be—too vile—I was jealous of her and I took advantage of my authority—it was all despicably unworthy of me, and we'll leave it at that. I have only one excuse, that I was in the power of something I knew nothing of. (*After a pause, with more emotion*) You have nothing to say—But then I do understand why, I do: for a man to have to listen to a declaration of love from a woman to whom he is indifferent—there can be nothing more painful, I am even grateful for your silence. You must feel intensely uncomfortable even in my presence—you have my permission to leave it at once, without formality—It seems that we two were never destined to know each other. Goodbye for ever.

SLOW DANCE ON THE KILLING GROUND

William Hanley

Rosie, a girl of nineteen, "singularly plain-looking with orange hair" and eyeglasses, has fainted at the doorstep of the store. Glas, the storekeeper, has brought her in and revived her. After some three-way dialogue (Randall, the young fugitive, is also there), Rosie explains why she is in the warehouse district at night. This monologue is almost comical. For more background on this play, see the introduction on page 143.

◆-◆•

ROSIE.
If you knew me better, you'd see that this is exactly the kind of thing that's likely to happen to me. (*She resumes combing of the wig.*) Getting knocked up, I mean. The point is it was my first time, I was a virgin before that. Wouldn't you know it, I'd get caught? Aside from everything else, I'm not lucky either. (*Glas puts butter in refrigerator.*) You see, if I was lucky, Harold and I could've succumbed to our silly little passion and that would've been that, the end of it. And New Rochelle, of all places. At least if

it'd been in some nice apartment in the Village, say, with the sounds coming through the window of traffic and people, the breeze blowing the curtain over the bed, like in the movies. But, no. I lost my virginity in the attic of an old house in New Rochelle. Harold's grandmother's house. On a rainy day in spring on the floor of the attic in his grandmother's house, listening to the rain on the roof, breathing the dust of old things. . . . And what comes next but his grandmother who was supposed to be in the city for the day. But instead she's suddenly standing in the door to the attic, attracted there, no doubt, by the scuffling sounds of the imminent consummation. So she's standing there, screaming: (*Rosie bangs on the table.*) "Stop that! Stop that this instant!" Needless to say, it was out of the question. Stopping. At that particular moment. I mean, sex is like a flight over the sea, one reaches the point of no return. . . . I guess it sounds funny now, but, you know, at the time . . . it was pretty rotten. Sordid, I mean . . . it wasn't at all the way it's supposed to be. (*Randall moves* D. *to chair* L.) And Harold, of all people. A girl finds herself in this predicament, this condition, she'd at least like to be able to think of the cause of it as being some clever, handsome guy with charm and experience, just returned from spending a year in Rome, say, on a Guggenheim fellowship. But Harold, . . . Harold is six foot two, about a hundred and twenty five pounds, tops, an Economics major at CCNY . . . That's about the best I'll ever be able to do, I know it. (*She smiles and snorts.*) Ever since I found out I was pregnant I've been walking around with a face down to here and my mother kept saying, "What's the matter with you, anyway, I just don't know what's gotten into you lately." So, finally, I told her: a kid named Harold, as a matter of fact. . . . (*Picks up bag and takes out compact. Wipes her mouth.*) Oh, well, I just keep telling myself: "Remember Rosie, like in the song . . . someday my prince will come . . . Snow White. . . ."

THE BEAUTIFUL PEOPLE

William Saroyan

This is an unusual, lyrical play about an unconventional but loving family that lives happily in an
old house near San Francisco. Agnes is the saint-
ly daughter who has just met a boy at the library
and is experiencing new emotions. In the following
scene, she talks to her father, a poet and scientist.
His lines, which are fondly supportive of her, are
deleted and marked by asterisks, and some stage
directions which are irrelevant to monologue are
also deleted. One line has been slightly altered for
continuity and is marked by brackets.

•—•

AGNES.
(AGNES *turns slowly and sees him. She tries to
smile—but the smile is full of sorrow*)
[What did I read at the Public Library?] The ency-
clopedia—about hummingbirds.

*　　*　　*

(*Crossing up Left of table*)

58

Yes, they can fly backwards. They're funny, too. They fight great big birds.

(Pause, suddenly; bitterly, turning away)

But I could have held ten doors for his one.

(Crosses down, looking away Left)

*   *   *

He was there first.

*   *   *

(By the doorway, leaning against the frame as she looks away)

The door's a big glass door that I never noticed before. And I never noticed before that with all the room in the world a space could still be made. If he wasn't waiting, he was there, with the space for me.

*   *   *

He almost cried, and then I almost cried, too. He didn't need to stand there that way, and neither did I, but that's what we did. I could have turned and walked away quickly. I *had been* walking quickly, but now I couldn't move. I wanted to, I guess, but I just couldn't. He was too alone, and then I was, too—and we just had to stay together.

*   *   *

(*Crosses up to him to Left of table. Puts her arms around his neck*)

First we went out on the steps of the library, but we just stood *there*, too. We got in the way of some people who were in a hurry. About eleven of them. They didn't like us. *Both* of us. They turned around and looked at us. There were other people coming and going, too, and we were still in the way. When we got out of their way we were facing the same direction—we weren't facing each other. We were together.

*   *   *

I couldn't think of anything to say. I didn't think I'd be able to speak English even—and I suppose I didn't, after we *did* talk—what we said was so foolish.

*   *   *

(*Kneeling at his Left*)

We could barely walk. He kept bumping into me and I kept bumping into him, and he kept saying excuse me and I kept saying oh that's all right. He stumbled, too, and said something about his shoes.

(*Her hand on his*)

*   *   *

He said they didn't fit.

*   *   *

(As she sits on floor, Left of him)

I don't understand anything. I began to see! I
didn't used to *see*. The street cars going by had
people in them suddenly. There have always been
people in street cars, but now they were beautiful
people. I never saw people that way before. They
were still sad and funny and worried-looking, but
now they were beautiful, too.

(On her knees)

We walked through the park and looked at everything together. It's not the same as looking at
things alone.

*   *   *

We looked at the pigeons, as if they had just come
down from the sky. As if there had never been birds
before. As if they came to be with us.

*   *   *

Oh, they're beautiful. They know people. They
live in buildings.

*   *   *

Oh, a sky full—a thousand, I guess. They circled
around and around. He pointed at them and said
pigeons. I knew they were pigeons, but when he

said they were—I *liked* him. And I knew what he meant, too.

*   *   *

I can't say what he meant, but I *know* what he meant. He didn't mean pigeons. He couldn't mean pigeons and say it so sadly. It was the same with everything else, too. Everybody in the street that we passed was new. They were like *him*. I felt sorry for them.

(*Sadly*)

I thought love would be another thing—not pity. Is pity love?

(*Angry, rises; crosses down Right above chair*)

He's bewildered and shy and full of terrible sorrow, and his shoes don't fit.

*   *   *

(*Slowly, as if she were seeking the words, leaning on back of chair down Right*)

I've waited every day—to meet one person in the world—who wouldn't offend me—and now that I've found him—instead of being heedless

(AGNES *crosses Left, two steps*)

and strong—and full of humor—he's sad. He could be barefooted for all I care, if he wouldn't be sad—because now I'm sad, too.

(Angry, comes forward a step.)

I won't allow it. Pity's no seed to throw among the living. It's for mice, whose littleness rejoices with it. I can't believe to live—to *really* live—is foolish or impossible.

(In soft voice)

Is it impossible, Father?

*   *   *

(Solemnly)

We're not apart from the others, Father. I *thought* we were, but we're not. We are *they*, and they are us. I know that now. I don't want the foolish life. I'll learn to live all over again, but if I can't live the life I know is mine to live, if everything is to be meaningless and foolish—

*   *   *

(LIGHTS in the room begin to dim down)

(Almost angry, turning away)

But I can't forget him. Why am I so afraid I'll never see him again?

(Almost breaking down. Tenderly)

Will I see him again, Father?

(WARN curtain)

CRIMES OF THE HEART

Beth Henley

This is what some might call a "woman's play" as it is about three sisters and written by a woman. The sisters have gathered at their family home for a reunion on the thirtieth birthday of the oldest sister, and they have an immediate crisis. The youngest, Babe, has just shot her husband, Zackery, after he discovered her with her friend, Willie Jay, a fifteen-year-old black boy.

— ◆ —

BABE.

And we were just standing around on the back porch playing with Dog. Well, suddenly, Zackery comes from around the side of the house. And he startled me 'cause he's supposed to be away at the office, and there he is coming from 'round the side of the house. Anyway, he says to Willie Jay, "Hey, boy, what are you doing back here?" And I said, "He's not doing anything. You just go on home, Willie Jay! You just run right on home." Well, before he can move, Zackery comes up and knocks him once right across the face and then shoves him down the porch steps, causing him to

65

skin up his elbow real bad on that hard concrete. Then he says, "Don't you ever come around here again, or I'll have them cut out your gizzard!" Well, Willie Jay starts crying, these tears come streaming down his face, then he gets up real quick and runs away with Dog following off after him. After that, I don't remember much too clearly; let's see . . . I went on into the living room, and I went right up to the davenport and opened the drawer where we keep the burglar gun . . . I took it out. Then I—I brought it up to my ear. That's right. I put it right inside my ear. Why, I was gonna shoot off my own head! That's what I was gonna do. Then I heard the back door slamming and suddenly, for some reason, I thought about mama . . . how she'd hung herself. And here I was about ready to shoot myself. Then I realized— that's right I realized how I didn't want to kill myself! And she—she probably didn't want to kill herself. She wanted to kill him, and I wanted to kill him, too. I wanted to kill Zackery, not myself 'Cause I—I wanted to live! So I waited for him to come on into the living room. Then I held out the gun, and I pulled the trigger, aiming for his heart, but getting him in the stomach. (*After a pause.*) It's funny that I really did that.

THE MIDDLE AGES

A. R. Gurney, Jr.

This is a play that goes back and forth in time. It opens in the elegant trophy room of an exclusive men's club where people are gathered after the funeral for Charles, a successful businessman and prominent member of the club. Charles' son, Barney, who has been away and returns for the funeral, remembers the many times he has spent in this room. He met Eleanor there when she was fourteen and shy and hiding her Jewish background. Years later, before she goes off to college, Eleanor becomes involved with Barney's brother. The following monologue follows a scene in which Barney, who has flunked out of college, tries to win Eleanor back. He has just gone into the bathroom and Eleanor talks to the bathroom door.

• ◆ •

ELEANOR.
The party's over, Barney. Everyone's leaving. I want to leave too. I don't want to stay here tonight, sweetie. Really. I don't (*She picks up a cookie, takes a bite, shakes her head, puts it down.*) I want my eight hours sleep. I want to go to Bermuda,

Barney. I want to lie around in the sun with
Billy and the whole gang. I want to play tennis
and hear the Whiffenpoofs at the Elbow Beach
Club. What's wrong with that, Barney? What's
wrong with people having fun? I love all that,
Barney. I love all those people. They're good-
looking, and they play games, and they know
all the lyrics to all the songs. (*Pause.*) You don't,
Barney. You can't sing and your tennis is terrible. You're bad for me, Barney. Mother says so,
and it's true. Every time I get with you, I get
all mixed up. That's why I arranged Bermuda.
You're too much for me, Barney. (*She blows out
the candles.*) I don't love you, Barney. I love Billy.
He was editor of the Year Book, and he's going
to Princeton in the fall, and he wants to be a
lawyer. You? You couldn't even stay in Frank-
lin and Marshall. What kind of a future would
I have with you? I want a home. I want a family. I've never had them. I'll never get them with
you, Barney. Barney? Did you hear me, Barney?

LILIOM

Ferenc Molnár

This second monologue from the play is a final good-bye by Julie to Liliom who has died. For more about this play, see the introduction on page 135.

• ◆ •

JULIE.

(JULIE *goes up, then comes down and takes* LILIOM'S *head in her hands.*)

Sleep, Liliom, sleep—it's no business of hers—I never even told you—but now I'll tell you—now I'll tell you—you bad, quick-tempered, rough, unhappy, wicked—*dear* boy—sleep peacefully, Liliom—they can't understand how I feel—I can't even explain to you—not even to you—how I feel—you'd only laugh at me—but you can't hear me any more. [*Between tender motherliness and reproach, yet with great love in her voice*] It was wicked of you to beat me—on the breast and on the head and face—but you're gone now.—You treated me badly—that was wicked of you—but sleep peacefully, Liliom—

you bad, bad boy, you—I love you—I never told you before—I was ashamed—but now I've told you—I love you. Liliom—sleep—my boy—sleep. [*She rises, gets Bible on table, sits down near the candle and reads softly to herself, so that, not the words, but an inarticulate murmur is heard. Matthew 5–1.* JULIE *murmurs.*] "And seeing the multitudes he went up into a mountain and when he was set his disciples came unto him and he opened his mouth and taught them saying: 'Blessed.' "

THE DAYS AND NIGHTS OF BEEBEE FENSTERMAKER

William Snyder

This comedy traces the life of a young woman over a period of three years. Beebee has left her hometown and with huge aspirations has gone to a large city. She has just moved in to her own rented apartment and has met Nettie Jo, a young neighbor who is helping her unpack. Here, Beebee explains her actions and feelings to the new friend. There are other monologues in this play for the young actress, as Beebee often talks to herself when lonely.

•━◆━•

BEEBEE.
I had to get out . . . My family life was very complicated. It's funny. On the one hand I believe my future's as bright as a button and nothin' can stand in my way. But sometimes when I'm home, a little devil gets next to me and says, "Beebee, you fly mighty high in your mind's eye, honey. But if you ever took the trouble to look two inches past your nose you'd see your life was signed, sealed and delivered before you were born. And it's got nothin' to do with love or

careers or flights of fancy." In one way or another my whole family's just waitin it out. They talk about what they're gonna do or what they should have done but they're just sittin there waitin for the axe to fall. And I must say, when I walk those streets in the dead of August, and the trees are dry as paper and the grass is burnt up crisp. And the sun's so hot and the air's so thick they shut out all the sounds. And I go to my grandmother's and see her moving from room to room, doin a little dab here and a little dab there. Waitin for night to come so she can sit on the porch and do somethin that's *nothin.* I think there's no comfort on this porch. There's no life in this town. There's no hope in this world. And God has long since passed away. Fall in line, Beebee, fall in line. In a hundred years who'll know the difference. Follow the path of least resistance, act out your part and *die.* But I said no! (*Crosses to bureau*) I'm not gonna sit around waitin for what I dread most to happen to me. I'm not gonna be one more ribbon on the maypole. (*Sets bureau.*) I'm cuttin loose! So last week when I got home from college—before I could even give myself time to think—I cashed in my six hundred dollars worth of savins bonds I'd received over the years as prize money—packed up Miss Amelia Earhart—(*Gets other suitcase and places it U. of bureau*) and high-tailed it down to the Trailways Bus Station and took off. So here I am, footloose and ready to tackle anything. I got money, an apartment and I'm free!

UNCLE VANYA

Anton Chekhov

In this play, a retired professor has just brought home his new young wife to his estate in Russia at the end of the nineteenth century. The unhappy wife, Elena, falls in love with Astroff, a doctor who visits often. Also in love with Astroff is Sonia, the professor's rather plain young daughter by a previous marriage. In the following garden scene Astroff and Sonia have finished a conversation and he has just left. She begins with a soliloquy about him and how she feels about herself. A few minutes later, Elena enters and the last part of Sonia's monologue is directed toward her. The intervening lines are deleted and marked by asterisks.

•◆•

SONIA.
(*Alone*): He didn't say anything to me. . . . His soul and heart are still hidden from me; but why do I feel so happy? (*Laughing from happiness*) I said to him: You are refined, noble, you have such a gentle voice. . . . Was it the wrong moment for just that? His voice trembles, caresses you— Here I feel him in the air. And when I told him

73

about a younger sister, he didn't understand. . . .
(*Wringing her hands*) Oh, how terrible it is that I
am not pretty! How terrible! And I know I am
not pretty. I know, I know. . . . Last Sunday as
we were leaving church, I heard them talking
about me and one woman said: "She is kind,
generous, but it's a pity she is not pretty." . . .
not pretty.

*   *   *

(*Laughing*): I have a silly face . . . haven't I? Here
he is, gone, and I keep hearing his voice and his
steps, and when I look at a dark window I see
his face there. Let me try to say what I mean—
but I can't talk so loud, I am ashamed. Let's go to
my room, there we'll talk. Do I seem silly to you?
Confess . . . tell me something about him. . . .

FUENTE OVEJUNA

Lope de Vega

From this typically flamboyant and violent play of the Spanish Golden Age, this monologue by a young girl, Laurencia, is a challenge to any young actress. It captures the age from which it comes, but cannot be played in an overly melodramatic way to modern audiences. In the town hall of Fuente Ovejuna, the name of her village, Laurencia passionately tells of her mistreatment. She talks to her father and other council members.

•◆•

LAURENCIA.
For many reasons—but chiefly because you let me be carried off by tyrants, by the traitors who rule over us, without attempting to avenge me. I was not yet Frondoso's wife, so you cannot say my husband should have defended me; this was my father's duty as long as the wedding had not been consummated; just as a nobleman about to purchase a jewel need not pay for it if it is lost while still in the merchant's keeping. From under your very eyes, Fernán Gómez dragged me to his house, and you let the wolf carry the sheep

like the cowardly shepherd you are. Can you
conceive what I suffered at his hands?—the dag-
gers pointed at my breast, the flatteries, threats,
insults, and lies used to make my chastity yield
to his fierce desires? Does not my bruised and
bleeding face, my dishevelled hair tell you anything? Are you not good men?—not fathers and
relatives? Do not your hearts sink to see me so
grievously betrayed? . . . Oh, you are sheep, how
well named the village of Fuente Ovejuna, Sheep
Well. Give me weapons and let me fight, since
you are but things of stone or metal, since you
are but tigers—no, not tigers, for tigers fiercely
attack those who steal their offspring, killing the
hunters before they can escape. You were born
timid rabbits; you are infidels, not Spaniards.
Chicken-hearted, you permit other men to abuse
your women. Put knitting in your scabbards—
what need have you of swords? By the living
God, I swear that your women will avenge
those tyrants and stone you all, you spinning
girls, you sodomites, you effeminate cowards.
Tomorrow deck yourselves in our bonnets and
skirts, and beautify yourselves with our cosmet-
ics. The Comendador will hang Frondoso from
a merlon of the tower, without let or trial, and
presently he will string you all up. And I shall be
glad—you race of half-men—that this honorable
town will be rid of effeminates, and the age of
Amazons will return, to the eternal amazement
of the world.

THE STAR-SPANGLED GIRL

Neil Simon

Neil Simon's comedies are as popular with actors as they are with audiences. The characters are grounded in reality and identifiable, and the humor comes out of the situations and funny lines. The actor should not try for humor; it is already there. In this play, two young men live in a studio apartment where they also publish a small magazine. Norman has fallen totally for Sophie, the girl who has just moved next door. As her following monologue attests, Norman is overly attentive. Sophie is from the South, an all-American girl, and genuinely upset as she talks to Norman in this scene. She is carrying a basket.

●—◆—●

SOPHIE.
Mr. Cornell, Ah have tried to be neighborly, Ah have tried to be friendly and Ah have tried to be cordial . . . Ah don't know what it is that you're tryin' to be. That first night Ah was appreciative that you carried mah trunk up the stairs . . . The fact that it slipped and fell five flights and smashed to pieces was not your fault . . . Ah

77

didn't even mind that personal message you painted on the stairs. Ah thought it was crazy, but sorta sweet. However, things have now gone too far . . . (*Goes down to the pole table*) Ah cannot accept gifts from a man Ah hardly know . . . (*Puts the basket on the pole table*) Especially canned goods. And Ah read your little note. Ah can guess the gist of it even though Ah don't speak Italian. This has got to stop, Mr. Cornell. Ah can do very well without you leavin' little chocolate-almond Hershey bars in mah mailbox—they melted yesterday, and now Ah got three gooey letters from home with nuts in 'em—and Ah can do without you sneakin' into mah room after Ah go to work and paintin' mah balcony without tellin' me about it. Ah stepped out there yesterday and mah slippers are still glued to the floor. And Ah can do without you tying big bottles of eau de cologne to mah cat's tail. The poor thing kept swishin' it yesterday and nearly beat herself to death . . . And most of all, Ah can certainly do without you watchin' me get on the bus every day through that high-powered telescope. You got me so nervous the other day Ah got on the wrong bus. In short, Mr. Cornell, and Ah don't want to have to say this again, *leave me ay-lone!*

A MIDSUMMER NIGHT'S DREAM

William Shakespeare

This is one of William Shakespeare's delightful comedies of young love and all its foibles. Helena is in love with Demetrius who seems to be in love with Hermia who, in turn, is in love with Lysander, with whom she has made plans to elope. Helena has just heard their marriage plan and makes one of her own to get her love back. As Puck says, "What fools these mortals be."

◆

HELENA.

How happy some o'er other some can be!
Through Athens I am thought as fair as she.
But what of that? Demetrius thinks not so;
He will not know what all but he do know.
And as he errs, doting on Hermia's eyes,
So I, admiring of his qualities.
Things base and vile, holding no quantity,
Love can transpose to form and dignity.
Love looks not with the eyes, but with the mind,
And therefore is winged Cupid painted blind.
Nor hath Love's mind of any judgment taste;

Wings, and no eyes, figure unheedy haste.
And therefore is Love said to be a child,
Because in choice he is so oft beguiled.
As waggish boys in game themselves forswear,
So the boy Love is perjured everywhere.
For ere Demetrius looked on Hermia's eyne,
He hailed down oaths that he was only mine;
And when this hail some heat from Hermia felt,
So he dissolved, and show'rs of oaths did melt.
I will go tell him of fair Hermia's flight.
Then to the wood will he to-morrow night
Pursue her; and for this intelligence
If I have thanks, it is a dear expense.
But herein mean I to enrich my pain,
To have his sight thither and back again.

(Exit)

LUDLOW FAIR

Lanford Wilson

This is a two-character, one-act comedy about two young women who share an apartment. It is a departure from the playright's other works, oftentimes about losers, drifters, and the misplaced. The following monologue by Rachel is from the beginning of the play. She waits for her roommate to come out of the bathroom. It is a humorous moment, though Rachel is serious in her attempt to analyze herself and what she has done. She agonizes over whether she should have called the police about a man she has been dating and who has stolen some money from her.

This monologue is followed by another, which occurs after a brief exchange from both sides of the bathroom door. A number of lines between Rachel and her roommate are deleted and marked by asterisks.

•◆•

RACHEL.
[*wandering around the room alone. She is restless; she looks at one thing and another. Finally, quite to herself*]. Oh, God; I think you're losing your

81

head. I think you're going stark raving insane
and you've got no one in this ever-loving world,
sweetheart, to blame except yourself. And maybe
Joe. But then. . . . Are you losing it? Hmm? Let's
see. [*She pinches herself firmly. For a full two seconds
she considers the effect. Matter-of-factly.*] Ouch!

*   *   *

[*Rubbing her arm.*] What a stupid thing to do.
That's no kind of test of insanity, anyway. That's
for drunkenness or sleepwalking or disorderly
conduct or something. How do you know if your
faculties are ebbing away from you, anyway?
[*Seriously considering.*] You go to an analyst,
what does he do? You lie down on the couch,
what does he do? Ha! No, a respectable analyst, what does he do? You lie—A quick little
word association. You can't give yourself a
word—well, why not? [*Sits quickly on the chair
at the desk.*] Ready? Ready. Very well, when I say
a word you come in with the very first word that
pops into your head. Yes, I understand. Very
well. [*Pause, tries for a split second to think of a
word. Finally.*] Word. [*Immediately answers.*] Word!
[*Blank pause.*] Dog. [*Absolutely blank for the count
of six. Aside.*] Oh, for Christ's sake. . . . [*Intense
concentration. Mumbles.*] Dog. [*Breaking away, then
firmly.*] Jesus Chri— DOG! [*Pause. With the same
studied intensity.*] CAT! [*Aside.*] For Christ's
sake—well, that's it—cat. Keep it up. Cat. [*Same
amount of pause between words, same intensity to
each word.*] Rat. Mouse. House. Rat. Dog. Cat.
Mouse. Louse. Bat. Pat. Fat. Louse. [*Breaking
away.*] Fat louse, Jesus Christ. Rat, cat, mouse,
louse, bat, house; you don't need an analyst

you need an exterminator. You can't associate with yourself. Even words. [*Calling to no one.*] Joe! [*Sees the dictionary on the desk, puts it in her lap.*] Well, why not? As long as you don't know the word that's coming up. Now the first word that pops into your head. [*Answering herself.*] Yes, I understand. [*She opens the book, looks down, closes it. Flatly.*] Knickerbocker! [*Sighs slowly, then with redetermination.*] All right, I'll play your stupid game with you. Holiday. Take that. [*Opens the book again. Looks more closely. Reading.*] Phen-a-kis-to-scope. [*Pause. Looking at it. Continues reading.*] "An instrument resembling the zoe-thrope in principle and use. One form consists of a disk with the figures arranged about the center, with radial slits—[*Aside*] Radial slits? [*Continues to read*] Radial slits through which the figures are viewed—[*Becoming amused.*]—by means of a mirror." [*Closing the dictionary.*] But what's it for? Phen-a-kis-to-scope. Very well. [*She gets up, wanders to the dresser. As though she were thinking.*] Phenakistoscope. Ah, ah . . . Zoethrope! Naturally. [*Sitting at the dresser, the dictionary open in front of her, she quite casually opens the nail polish and pours an amount on one page, shuts the dictionary firmly, props it open again, like an easel against the back of the vanity. Studies it carefully from some distance.*] Ah . . . Oh, ah . . . A tree. [*Aside.*] A tree. That couldn't possibly mean anything. [*Looks back at it, studying.*] Ah. Ah. Your trouble is you have no imagination, Rachel. You're not nuts, you're just dull. Okay . . . Ah. An ostrich. That's a little better. An ostrich. Eating. [*Considering her progress.*] An ostrich, huh? That's vaguely phallic, you know. Well, vaguely. [*Shutting the book.*] That's the trouble with those things, when they start working you're in trouble. [*She gets up, carrying the book, rubs her arm.*] If you don't learn to stop pinching yourself.

* * *

[*She lays the book back on the dresser, wanders about.*] There's nothing wrong with you, Rachel, except you're given to talking to yourself—driven to talking to yourself. [*Falls down on her bed, stretched out, looking up blankly.*] Long pointless conversations before retiring. Well, doctor—it's this way. Joe turned out to be a rat. But then I think I knew that before he turned out. [*Props herself on one elbow.*] I was just sitting home saying to myself, Rachel, you have got to get yourself a new phenakistoscope. The one you've got is just a mess. The radial slits are all shot. And when the radial slits are shot, there's just no hope. For a phenakistoscope. Or anything else, for that matter. [*She sits on the side of the bed, face in hands, near the point of crying for just a second, then pulls out of it and gets up.*] Oh dear, oh dear, oh dear, oh dear. Joe. Joe. Joe. Where did you go? [*Pause*]. All the way to . . . [*Breaks off. Walks to dresser, sees dictionary.*] What have you been doing? Testing your sanity again, huh? What are you crazy or something? There's nothing wrong with you. [*Sees her reflection in the mirror. Pleased but critical.*] Five foot two. Five foot six, actually: Girls are bigger than ever. Lovely dark hair, fine hair. Opalescent skin. Lovely hips. Fine breasts. Nice legs. Nice, hell, great legs. Not bad ears; good hands. Slightly blah eyes, frankly; but then you can't have everything. What you are is probably a louse. A fool, of course, and a probable louse. Moral to a fault. And where you are a probable louse, Joe is a first-class, A-one, definite louse without a doubt, and it is good to have a first-class, definite louse out of your hair. [*She lights a cigarette.*] Four hundred and thirty-six dollars. [*Takes a puff; exhales.*] And thirty-eight cents. [*Wandering about.*] And several Government checks, like thirty, say. And about twenty-odd forgeries, and about four cars, and four hundred and thirty-six dollars and thirty-eight cents.

*   *   *

[*without paying attention. To herself*]. Oh, God. [*Sees herself in the mirror.*] Girl, you are a mess. Just a mess. [*Pause.*]

LUDLOW FAIR

Lanford Wilson

In this play, Agnes is described as "no raving beauty" but "a great deal of fun." This is a comedic monologue by Agnes. She is suffering a cold, setting her hair, and talking to her roommate who is in bed and presumably asleep. For more about this play, see page 81.

•—◆—•

AGNES.

Well sleep it off. I don't know why you should worry any more about Joe than you did about whoever it was before. You've got to admit the pattern is evident there somewhere. Maybe you should really go to an analyst, you know? No joke. You probably have some kind of problem there somewhere. I mean no one's normal. He's bound to find something. It might keep you away from dictionaries, you know? Jesus. Well, I say if it helps, do it. To hell with how funny it looks. God knows I'd like to find—I'm absolutely getting pneumonia. [*Gets up to get the box of Kleenex and carries it back to the vanity, talking all the while.*] I'm going to be a mess tomorrow. I probably

won't make it to work, let alone lunch. A casual
lunch, my God. I wonder what he'd think—stupid
Charles—if he knew I was putting up my hair for
him; catching pneumonia. No lie, I can't wait till
summer to see what kind of sunglasses he's going
to pop into the office with. Probably those World's
Fair charmers. A double unisphere. [*Turns.*] Are
you going to sleep? [*Pause. No reply.*] Well, crap.
[*Turning back to mirror.*] I may be tendering my
notice, anyway. You've gone through six men
while I sit around and turn to fungus. It's just
not a positive atmosphere for me, honey. Not
quite. You're out with handsome Val or someone and I'm wondering if the boss's skinny, bony
son will come up to the water cooler if I. . . . [*Trails
off, becomes interested in the roller. Now to someone—
as at dinner.*] No. No Stroganoff. No, I'm on a diet.
[*Correcting herself.*] No. I will not admit that. Good
or bad if he says Stroganoff and baked potatoes it's
Stroganoff and baked potatoes. And sour cream.
And beer. He's probably on a diet himself. He
could fill out, God knows. [*Turning to* RACHEL.]
You know what Charles looks like? [*Pause.*] He
looks like one of those little model men you make
out of pipe cleaners when you're in grade school.
[*Turning.*] Remember those? If I ever saw Charles
without his clothes, he's so pale and white, I swear
to God I'd laugh myself silly. He's Jewish, too. I'll
bet his mother is a nervous wreck. I'll bet she
thinks every woman on the block is pointing
at her. Look, there goes Mrs. Schwartz; starv-
ing her children to death. Poor Charles. Shakes
like a leaf. Of course Mrs. Schwartz wouldn't
admit that either. No woman would admit her
son was nervous; what's he got to be nervous
about? The nerve of being nervous. My kid broth-

er got an ulcer, my mother went to bed for three weeks, totally destroyed. Of course she spent about two thirds of her life totally destroyed. Upset—bawling. Weeks on end sometimes. My brother was great. He never paid the slightest attention to her; she'd get one of her spells and run off to bed bawling, it never bothered him for a minute. Off she'd go, the slightest provocation. Eric would say, "Mother's bedridden with the piss-offs again." I used to come home for a holiday or something and I'd say where's Mom and Eric would say, "Oh, she's bedridden with the piss-offs again." [*As if directly to someone, over lunch. Casually.*] You know, Charles, you've got nice eyes. You really have. Deep. I like brown eyes for a man. I don't like blue eyes, they always look weak or weepy. Either that or cold. You know? Brown eyes are warm; that's good. They're gentle. [*Quickly.*] Not weak, but gentle. [*Half to herself. Lightly.*] I used to want to have a girl; a little girl with blue eyes. For a girl that's good. So I used to always picture—God, idealize, really—very heavy-set, blond men. Swiss types, you know. [*Back to Charles.*] But a son I'd want to have brown eyes. That's better for boys. [*Looks at the sleeve of her robe.*] You think? [*Almost embarrassed.*] I don't know any more— Oh, yes; I got it at Saks. It was on sale, I believe. [*Breaking off, disgusted.*] Now, what the hell does he care where I got it? And it wasn't on sale, knucklehead. And it wasn't Saks. [*Concentrating on her hair.*] It was Bonds. Not that he'd know the damn difference. [*She drops a roller, it bounces across the floor. She picks up another without even looking after the first one.*] Fuck. [*Finishing her hair.*] I've got to quit saying that.

[*This last said without listening to herself; second nature. She picks up a jar of cold cream, slowly, distantly, applies a dab to her lower lip. Pause. She sits still, staring off vacantly. A full thirty-second pause.*]

IPHIGENIA IN AULIS

Euripides

This was Euripides last play and is based on the ancient Homeric legend of Agamemnon's sacrifice of his daughter Iphigenia to the goddess Artemis in order to ensure the Greek ships favorable winds on their way to Troy. Because Euripides created his characters in a more human, rather than legendary way, Iphigenia is portrayed as girlish, affectionate, and as a young woman who wants to live. The scene takes place at the tent of Agamemnon on the shore of Aulis Gulf where he has sent for his daughter on a false pretext. When Iphigenia discovers the truth, she pleads for her life.

•◆•

IPHIGENIA.

O my father—
If I had the tongue of Orpheus
So that I could charm with song the stones to
Leap and follow me, or if my words could
Quite beguile anyone I wished—I'd use
My magic now. But only with tears can I
Make arguments and here I offer them.

90

O Father,
My body is a suppliant's tight clinging
To your knees. Do not take away this life
Of mine before its dying time. Nor make me
Go down under the earth to see the world
Of darkness, for it is sweet to look on
The day's light.
I was first to call you father,
You to call me child. And of your children
First to sit upon your knees. We kissed
Each other in our love. "O child,"
You said, "surely one day I shall see you
Happy in your husband's home. And like
A flower blooming for me and in my honor."
Then as I clung to you and wove my fingers
In your beard, I answered, "Father, you,
Old and reverent then, with love I shall
Receive into my home, and so repay you
For the years of trouble and your fostering
Care of me." I have in memory all these words
Of yours and mine. But you, forgetting,
Have willed it in your heart to kill me.
no—by Pelops
And by Atreus, your father, and
By my mother who suffered travail
At my birth and now must suffer a second
Time for me! Oh, oh—the marriage
Of Paris and Helen—Why must it touch
My life? Why must Paris be my ruin?
Father, look at me, and into my eyes;
Kiss me, so that if my words fail,
And if I die, this thing of love I may
Hold in my heart and remember.

ALBUM

David Rimmer

Four fourteen-year-olds, two girls and two boys, are alone in one of their homes. They have just been playing strip poker, and the girls have fled to a bedroom in embarrassment and locked the door. The scenes alternate back and forth from the bedroom, where the girls are talking about boys, and the hall outside the bedroom, where the boys are talking about girls. Trish, who is the shyer of the two girls, has a crush on Brian, one of the singers of the Beach Boys, and tells Peggy about it.

•—◆—•

TRISH.
It's always right before I go to sleep. I take my radio from under the pillow, and I put it away, and I lie there and close my eyes . . . Sorta like dreaming but I'm awake too . . . We're walking on the beach, me and Brian, not holding hands or anything, just walking. The sun's going down over the ocean, there's nobody else there, you can hear the waves. Then we stop, right at the edge. I look at his face, and I know he's gonna touch me, I can feel it, like a fire. I look at the

sky behind him and I can see the stars. I can
count them, it's not even dark. Then he says,
"Listen . . ." And I close my eyes, and I hear
the ocean, and I feel it inside me, tingling, and
warm, and I can't wait for him to touch me . . .
The beach is in California. Can you imagine? The
Pacific Ocean . . . I can't even think of it, it's so
far. Think we'll ever get to go there, Peg? I'd
give anything to go . . .

FOR COLORED GIRLS WHO HAVE CONSIDERED SUICIDE WHEN THE RAINBOW IS ENUF

Ntozake Shange

This unconventional and moving play is called a "choreopoem" by its author. Seven black women, each wearing a different color, move in dancelike motions and share their lives and feelings. The following is a humorous, sad, and difficult monologue by the Lady in Blue as she apparently addresses a man she once loved; she speaks directly to the audience.

●━◆━●

LADY IN BLUE.

one thing i dont need
is any more apologies
i got sorry greetin me at my front door
you can keep yrs
i dont know what to do wit em
they dont open doors
or bring the sun back
they dont make me happy
or get a mornin paper
didnt nobody stop usin my tears to wash cars
cuz a sorry

i am simply tired
of collectin
i didnt know
i was so important toyou'
i'm gonna haveta throw some away
i cant get to the clothes in my closet
for alla the sorries
i'm gonna tack a sign to my door
leave a message by the phone
'if you called
to say yr sorry
call somebody
else
i dont use em anymore'
i let sorry/didnt meanta/& how cd i
know abt that
take a walk down a dark &
musty street in brooklyn
i'm gonna do exactly what i want to
& i wont be sorry for none of it
letta sorry soothe yr soul/i'm gonna soothe mine

you were always inconsistent
doin somethin & then bein sorry
beatin my heart to death
talkin bout you sorry
well
i will not call
i'm not goin to be nice
i will raise my voice
& scream & holler
& break things & race the engine
& tell all yr secrets bout yrself to yr face
& i will list in detail everyone of
my wonderful lovers

& their ways
i will play oliver lake
loud
& i wont be sorry for none of it

i loved you on purpose
i was open on purpose
i still crave vulnerability & close talk
& i'm not even sorry bout you bein sorry
you can carry all the guilt & grime ya wanna
just dont give it to me
i cant use another sorry
next time
you should admit
you're mean/low-down/triflin/
& no count straight out
steada bein sorry alla the time
enjoy bein yrself

KENNEDY'S CHILDREN

Robert Patrick

This is a play of monologues. The action takes place in a bar on the lower East Side of New York on an afternoon in 1974. Five young people are sitting alone either at the tables or the bar and speaking to no one in particular as they remember the 1960s. Because they do not relate well to each other but are caught up in their own memories, the monologues are not intended to explain or communicate. Instead, they show the characters trying to come to grips with their own feelings. The student actor would be well advised to read this entire play for the gold mine of monologues.

The following monologue is delivered by Carla, a confused young woman with a not-so-savory past. Although she finds her self-deprecation humourous, Carla would not want to be considered pathetic or victimized.

•——◆——•

CARLA.

I threw myself, at fifteen, with a sense of mission so strong it would have made Joan of Arc's look like a whim, I threw myself into Manhattan's

97

lap—head first. I bought a subscription to *Show Business* and a subscription to *Backstage* and I borrowed fifteen cents for the subway and I went to all the casting calls. There were an awful lot of pretty girls in New York then. We'd all line up, all pert and prettified, and do whatever we were told to do, like good bad little girls. "Stand up straight." "Swell your chests." "Smile." "Look left." "Look right." And I'd look left and I'd see the backs of the heads of a lot of pretty girls looking left. And I'd look right and see the backs of the heads of a lot of pretty girls looking right. So, I got a job as a go-go girl at the Metropole. We still wore bras then. I had resume photographs made and sent them out to all the important agents. I met an awful lot of important agents. I went out with several of them—once. I kept abreast of the very latest styles. I found a guy who'd do my hair for free if I'd do a number with him in the back of his shop. Only we weren't yet calling it "doing a number." We called it "pussycatting." We were—what *was* that word? Oh, yes—"swingers." He was young and cute. I was young and cute. It was an exchange of favors. It was also an exchange of favors with the guy who supplied me with hats. And—why not admit it?—with the woman who gave me jewelry. We were young professionals helping each other. Those people were getting an awful lot of that kind of help from girls like me. And we were getting very professional. Well! I never walked the streets. And I never worked a bar. And I never rode around Times Square in a taxicab wearing nothing but a mink coat. Although they'd probably welcome that as a return to good breeding, compared with the junkies who are doing the Times

Square whoring nowadays. Because that's what we were—rolled-up copy of *Backstage* or not—*whores!* How do you think I got that job at the Metropole? Through character references?

WHERE HAS TOMMY FLOWERS GONE?

Terrence McNally

Nedda is a young girl who now lives with Tommy. In the following scene, she stops playing her cello to address the audience. For more about this unconventional play, see the introduction on page 187.

•◆•

NEDDA.
I'd like to ask Tommy if he loves me. I wonder what he'd say. I'm sorry, but I'm a very conventional budding girl cellist from Tampa, Florida, that way. Tommy's from St. Petersburg. Small world, isn't it? I grew up thinking life could be very nice if you just let it. I still do. It's certainly full of surprises and most of them are good. Like my music. That happened when I was ten years old and went to my first concert. I came home in a dream. Or like Tommy Flowers! That happened . . . well, you *saw* where that happened and we came home in a cab Tommy didn't pay for. I love my music. Whenever I get the teeniest bit depressed I think about it and I'm all right again. The notes are hard for

me, I can't always play them at first, but if practice makes perfect then I'm going to be a very good cellist one day. That's what I want. And now there's Tommy. Someone I hadn't counted on at all. A small world but so many different people in it! I don't know what Tommy wants, so I have to play it by ear with him. That's hard for me and I'm pretty smart about men. It's not like practicing my music; Tommy has to help, too. And which is real or which is realer? All these little, wonderful, difficult notes some man wrote once upon a time somewhere or me, right now, in a whole other place, trying to play them and wanting to ask Tommy Flowers if he loves me and wanting him to answer, "I love you, Nedda Lemon"? They're both real. I don't want to change the world. I just want to be in it with someone. For someone with such a sour name, I could be a very happy girl.

MONOLOGUES
FOR YOUNG
MEN

ALBUM

David Rimmer

This scene takes place in Boo's room at school two years after the previous scene. Boo is sixteen, fast-talking, and fidgety. A few short lines by his friend, Billy, are deleted and marked by asterisks. For more information about this play, see page 92.

•◆•

BOO.
Hey . . . I just remembered this dream I had last night.

*   *   *

I was at this big posh party in London, at this really rich house. It was really high up, and there were these big picture windows, you could see the river and all the lights of the town. I was with a girl—you know who it was? Trish.

*   *   *

We were just lookin' out the window . . . And all these rich little old ladies started runnin' around

105

all over the place, all excited, sayin' Mick Jagger's coming, isn't that wonderful, Mick Jagger's coming. They came up to us and they told us be careful cause the latest thing in London now was sadism, and Mick was really into it. Then they flitted away, laughin' and eatin' *hors d'oeuvres* and stuff, and everybody was just waitin' for Mick to show up. Finally he did, he just walked right in, Marianne Faithfull was with him—she had purple hair. And this whole crowd of little old ladies swarmed all around him. They introduced me to him, and he was incredibly scary-looking, his face, he really made me scared just lookin' at him. He had lipstick on and make-up and he was dressed like a woman, but it was more like he really *was* a woman, a woman and a man at the same time. All of a sudden he started pullin' my hair, really vicious, and he had these bracelets on that were made outta spikes, they jabbed into me, I saw drops of blood drippin' off 'em like a horror movie. I screamed or somethin', I just ran away I was so scared. I ended up in this room away from the party, nobody around, and I saw this guy sittin' on a couch, just sittin' there by himself, really quiet, watchin' TV. I sat down and watched the TV for a couple of minutes, then I turned and looked at the guy . . . and it was Dylan.

THE CORN IS GREEN

Emlyn Williams

This is a dramatic and touching play that takes place in a small mining village in a remote Welsh countryside. The set is a large living room, which Englishwoman Miss Moffat has inherited the house and turned into a classroom. Miss Moffat discovers ability and creativity in a young coal miner, Morgan, and tutors him with intense dedication. Morgan is alternately enthusiastic about learning and rebellious as he begins to feel that his education is alienating him from his community. The following is a conversation between student and teacher with Miss Moffat's lines deleted and marked by asterisks.

•◆•

MORGAN.
  I shall not need a nail file in the coal mine.

*   *   *

  (*Turns to her.*) I am going back to the coal mine.

*   *   *

I do not want to learn Greek, nor to pronounce any long English words, nor to keep my hands clean.

*   *   *

Because . . . because (*Leans over, both hands on table*.)—I was born in a Welsh hayfield when my mother was helpin' with the harvest—and I always lived in a little house with no stairs, only a ladder—and no water—and until my brothers was killed I never sleep except three in a bed. I know that is terrible grammar but it is true.

*   *   *

The last two years I have not had no proper talk with English chaps in the mine because I was so busy keepin' this old grammar in its place. Tryin' to better myself . . . tryin' to better myself, the day and the night! . . . You cannot take a nail file into the "Gwesmor Arms" public bar!

*   *   *

I have been there every afternoon for a week, spendin' your pocket money, and I have been there now, (*Rises*.) and that is why I can speak my mind! (*Two steps* L.)

*   *   *

Because you are not interested in me.

*   *   *

How can you be interested in a machine that you put a penny in and if nothing comes out you give it a good shake? "Evans, write me an essay; Evans, get up and bow; Evans, what is a subjunctive?" My name is Morgan Evans, and all my friends call me Morgan, and if there is anything gets on the wrong side of me it is callin' me Evans! . . . And do you know what they call me in the Village? (*Crosses front couch* L.) *Ci bach yr ysgol!* The schoolmistress's little dog! What has (*Crosses to her*.) it got to do with you if my nails are dirty? Mind your own business! (*Sits sofa, head in hand, faces* L.)

THE CORN IS GREEN

Emlyn Williams

In spite of Morgan's sporadic resistance to his education, which is expressed in the previous monologue, he has studied hard for three years with Miss Moffat and just returned from taking entrance examinations at Oxford. He is describing his experiences there to his teacher, whose lines are deleted and marked by asterisks. Morgan is aglow. For more about this play, see the introduction on page 107.

•—◆—•

MORGAN.
I was terrible—terribly nervous. My collar stud flew off, and I had to hold on to my collar with one hand, and he did not seem impressed with me at all. . . . He was very curious about you. (*Rises.*) Did you know there was an article in the Morning Post about the school?

* * *

The other candidates. They appeared to be brilliant—I had never thought they would be, somehow! Two from Eton and one from Harrow, one of them very rich. I had never thought a scholarship man might be richer. He had his own servant.

* * *

And the servant looked so like my father I thought it was at first . . . (*Crosses upstage* R. *of small desk* L.C.) And as I was leaving, the examiners appeared to be sorry for me in some way, and I received the impression that I had failed. I—

* * *

If I have failed? (*Crosses via* C. *to front of couch.*) Don't speak about it!

* * *

I know, but I have *been* to Oxford, and come back, since then! I have come back—from the world! Since the day I was born, I have been a prisoner behind (*Sits* L. *end of couch.*) a stone wall, and now somebody has given me a leg-up to have a look at the other side . . . they cannot drag me back again, they cannot, they *must* give me a push and send me over!

* * *

That is just it! I *can* talk, now! The three days I have been there, I have been talking my head off!

* * *

That's just it again—it would be everything I
need, everything! Starling and I spent three hours
one night discussin' the law—Starling, you know,
the brilliant one. . . . The words came pouring out
of me—all the words that I had learnt and written
down and never spoken—I suppose I was talking
nonsense, but I was at least holding a conversation! I suddenly realized that I had never done
it before—I had never been *able* to do it. (*With
a strong Welsh accent.*) "How are you, Morgan?
Nice day, Mr. Jones! Not bad for the harvest!"—a
vocabulary of twenty words; all the thoughts that
you have given to me were being stored away as if
they were always going to be useless—locked up
and rotting away—a lot of questions with nobody
to answer them, a lot of statements with nobody to
contradict them . . . and there I was with Starling,
nineteen to the dozen. I came out of his rooms that
night, and I walked down the High. That's their
High Street, you know.

*   *   *

I looked up, and there was a moon behind Magd—
Maudlin. Not the same moon I have seen over
the Nant, a different face altogether. Everybody
seemed to be walking very fast, with their gowns
on, in the moonlight; the bells were ringing, and
I was walking faster than anybody and I felt—
well, the same as on the rum in the old days!

*   *   *

All of a sudden, with one big rush, against that
moon, and against that High Street . . . I saw this
room; you and me sitting here studying, and all

those books—and everything I have ever learnt from those books, and from you, was lighted up—like a magic lantern—ancient Rome, Greece, Shakespeare, Carlyle, Milton . . . everything had a meaning because I was in a new world—my world! And so it came to me why you worked like a slave to make me ready for this scholarship . . . I've finished.

THE DAYS AND NIGHTS OF BEEBEE FENSTERMAKER

William Snyder

A young man with an Arkansas accent has shown up at Beebee's apartment, believing that a friend of his lives there. Beebee, alone on her birthday, has invited him in, and in this scene, he talks about himself. A few of Beebee's short intervening lines and some dialogue between the two are deleted and marked by asterisks. For more background on this play, see the previous introduction on page 71.

◆—◆

BOB.

My name is Bob Smith, care of Claude and Esther Berry Smith, Box 231, Hughes, Arkansas. I'm twenty-five years old and I have an eighth grade education.

* * *

My Daddy run me clean out of town. Bought me a one way ticket on a Trailways Bus. Told me he'd buy me a one way ticket to anyplace in the U.S.A. Even rode with me as far as Le-Hi (*Pronounced Lee-High.*) to make sure I didn't pull a fast one and slip back after sundown. He said Hughes wasn't big enough for the both of us. Hughes is tee-ninecy all right. But I didn't think it was that small. Last I seen of my Daddy was when the bus pulled into Le-Hi. He got off the bus and bought me a Dr. Pepper and this comic book. (*He pulls comic book from hip pocket.*) He said, "Well, so long, Bob. I'll see you in the funny papers." Before I could even say anything he skipped across the highway and was thumbin a ride back to Hughes. That was the last I seen of my Daddy. The very last I seen of him before he took off for Hughes. I bet he was back there before supper. I know he's back there by now.

*   *   *

(*Pleasantly.*) (*He looks at kitchen table.*) I wonder what Momma and Daddy had for supper? Fried chicken most likely. I sure do love fried chicken. I sure do miss Hughes. I never been no further than Blackfish Lake cept the time Momma and Daddy took me up to hear Reverend Moore preach a revival at Proctor. Momma's a bug on religion, but old Reverend Moore's one somebody sure igged her. Reverend Moore's the shoutin foot stompin kind of religion, and Momma's is the toe the line, hoe the row kind. They don't even sing in Momma's church. It was started up right there in Hughes by Reverend Bitsie Trotter. He does odd jobs with a pick-up truck during the week. Folks said the reason he didn't allow singin was cause he couldn't carry a tune.

THE GLASS MENAGERIE

Tennessee Williams

This lyrical, autobiographical play made Tennessee Williams known to an adoring public. Set in St. Louis, Amanda, described as a mother "clinging frantically to another time and place," is struggling to keep her family intact after her husband has deserted them. Her son Tom is a frustrated writer, miserable working in a shoe warehouse. He finds some outlet for his unhappiness by drinking and going to the movies. In the following scene, he has just staggered home late and is met by his sister, Laura, a lame, shy girl and owner of a glass menagerie. Laura's lines and one reply by Tom are deleted and marked by asterisks.

•—◆—•

The interior of the apartment is dark. There is a faint light in the alley. A deep-voiced bell in a church is tolling the hour of five.

Tom appears at the top of the alley. After each solemn boom of the bell in the tower, he shakes a little noisemaker or rattle as if to express the tiny spasm of man in contrast to the sustained

116

power and dignity of the Almighty. This and the unsteadiness of his advance make it evident that he has been drinking. As he climbs the few steps to the fire escape landing light steals up inside. Tom fishes in his pockets for his door key, removing a motley assortment of articles in the search, including a shower of movie ticket stubs and an empty bottle. At last he finds the key, but just as he is about to insert it, it slips from his fingers. He strikes a match and crouches below the door.

TOM.

There was a very long program. There was a Garbo picture and a Mickey Mouse and a travelogue and a newsreel and a preview of coming attractions. And there was an organ solo and a collection for the Milk Fund—simultaneously—which ended up in a terrible fight between a fat lady and an usher!

* * *

And, oh, I forgot! There was a big stage show! The headliner on this stage show was Malvolio the Magician. He performed wonderful tricks, many of them, such as pouring water back and forth between pitchers. First it turned to wine and then it turned to beer and then it turned to whisky. I know it was whisky it finally turned into because he needed somebody to come up out of the audience to help him, and I came up— both shows! It was Kentucky Straight Bourbon. A very generous fellow, he gave souvenirs. [*He pulls from his back pocket a shimmering rainbow-colored scarf.*] He gave me this. This is his magic scarf. You can have it, Laura. You wave it over a canary cage and you get a bowl of goldfish. You wave it over the goldfish bowl and they fly away canaries. . . . But the wonderfullest trick of all was the coffin trick. We nailed him into a coffin and he got out of the coffin without removing one nail. [*He has come inside.*] There is a trick that would come in handy for me—get me out of this two-by-four situation! [*He flops onto the bed and starts removing his shoes.*]

* * *

You know it don't take much intelligence to get yourself into a nailed-up coffin, Laura. But who in hell ever got himself out of one without removing one nail?

THE GLASS MENAGERIE

Tennessee Williams

◆—◆—◆

The following is an emotional scene between Tom and his mother, Amanda. His sister, Laura, watches on. Mother and son have been arguing. She has just said she is at the end of her patience when Tom plunges in, loses his temper, and tells her off. Her lines have been deleted and marked by asterisks; Tom rants and then exits furiously.

•—◆—•

TOM.

What do you think I'm at? Aren't I supposed to have any patience to reach the end of, Mother? I know, I know. It seems unimportant to you, what I'm *doing*—what I *want* to do—having a little *difference* between them! You don't think that—

*   *   *

Listen! You think I'm crazy about the *warehouse*? [*He bends fiercely toward her slight figure.*] You think I'm in love with the Continental Shoemakers? You think I want to spend fifty-five *years* down there

119

in that—*celotex interior!* with—*fluorescent*—*tubes!*
Look! I'd rather somebody picked up a crowbar
and battered out my brains—than go back morn-
ings! I *go!* Every time you come in yelling that
Goddamn *"Rise and Shine!" "Rise and Shine!"* I
say to myself, "How *lucky dead* people are!" But
I get up. I *go!* For sixty-five dollars a month I give
up all that I dream of doing and being *ever!* And
you say self—*self's* all I ever think of. Why, listen,
if self is what I thought of, Mother, I'd be where
he is—GONE! [*He points to his father's picture.*] As
far as the system of transportation reaches! [*He
starts past her. She grabs his arm.*] Don't grab at
me, Mother!

*   *   *

I'm going to the *movies!*

*   *   *

[*Tom crouches toward her, overtowering her tiny
figure.*]

I'm going to opium dens! Yes, opium dens, dens of
vice and criminals' hangouts, Mother. I've joined
the Hogan Gang, I'm a hired assassin, I carry a
tommy gun in a violin case! I run a string of cat
houses in the Valley! They call me Killer, Killer
Wingfield, I'm leading a double-life, a simple,
honest warehouse worker by day, by night a
dynamic *czar* of the *underworld, Mother.* I go to
gambling casinos, I spin away fortunes on the
roulette table! I wear a patch over one eye and a
false mustache, sometimes I put on green whisk-
ers. On those occasions they call me—*El Diablo!*

Oh, I could tell you many things to make you sleepless! My enemies plan to dynamite this place. They're going to blow us all sky-high some night! I'll be glad, very happy, and so will you! You'll go up, up on a broomstick, over Blue Mountain with seventeen gentlemen callers! You ugly—babbling old—witch . . .

[*He goes through a series of violent, clumsy movements, seizing his overcoat, lunging to the door, pulling it fiercely open. His arm catches in the sleeve of the coat as he struggles to pull it on. For a moment he is pinioned by the bulky garment. With an outraged groan he tears the coat off again, splitting the shoulder of it, and hurls it across the room. It strikes against the shelf of Laura's glass collection, and there is a tinkle of shattering glass.*]

THE GLASS MENAGERIE

Tennessee Williams

Tom, besides being a character in this play, also functions as the narrator. The following is an example of this role as he steps out of the action and addresses the audience. For background on this play, see the introduction on page 116.

•◆•

TOM.

[*to the audience*]: Across the alley from us was the Paradise Dance Hall. On evenings in spring the windows and doors were open and the music came outdoors. Sometimes the lights were turned out except for a large glass sphere that hung from the ceiling. It would turn slowly about and filter the dusk with delicate rainbow colors. Then the orchestra played a waltz or a tango, something that had a slow and sensuous rhythm. Couples would come outside, to the relative privacy of the alley. You could see them kissing behind ash pits and telephone poles. This was the compensation for lives that passed like mine, without any change or adventure. Adventure and change were imminent in this year. They were waiting around the corner for all these kids. Suspended in the mist over Berchtesgaden, caught in the folds of Chamberlain's umbrella. In Spain there was Guernica! But here there was only hot swing music and liquor, dance halls, bars, and movies, and sex that hung in the gloom like a chandelier and flooded the world with brief, deceptive rainbows. . . . All the world was waiting for bombardments!

THE GLASS MENAGERIE

Tennessee Williams

A young man has been invited to dinner by Tom at Amanda's insistence in order to meet his sister Laura. He was an old acquaintance of Laura's in high school. He was very popular and now works with Tom at the warehouse. In the following scene, Jim and Laura have been left alone in the living room and he is talking to her. Her two short lines have been deleted and marked by asterisks. For more background on this play, see page 116.

◆

JIM.

[*abruptly*] You know what I judge to be the trouble with you? Inferiority complex! Know what that is? That's what they call it when someone low-rates himself! I understand it because I had it, too. Although my case was not so aggravated as yours seems to be. I had it until I took up public speaking, developed my voice, and learned that I had an aptitude for science. Before that time I never thought of myself as being outstanding in any way whatsoever! Now I've never made a regular study of it, but I have a friend

124

who says I can analyze people better than doctors that make a profession of it. I don't claim that to be necessarily true, but I can sure guess a person's psychology, Laura! [*He takes out his gum.*] Excuse me, Laura. I always take it out when the flavor is gone. I'll use this scrap of paper to wrap it in. I know how it is to get it stuck on a shoe. [*He wraps the gum in paper and puts it in his pocket.*] Yep—that's what I judge to be your principal trouble. A lack of confidence in yourself as a person. You don't have the proper amount of faith in yourself. I'm basing that fact on a number of your remarks and also on certain observations I've made. For instance that clumping you thought was so awful in high school. You say that you even dreaded to walk into class. You see what you did? You dropped out of school, you gave up an education because of a clump, which as far as I know was practically non-existent! A little physical defect is what you have. Hardly noticeable even! Magnified thousands of times by imagination! You know what my strong advice to you is? Think of yourself as *superior* in some way!

*   *   *

Why, man alive, Laura! Just look about you a little. What do you see? A world full of common people! All of 'em born and all of 'em going to die! Which of them has one-tenth of your good points! Or mine! Or anyone else's, as far as that goes—gosh! Everybody excels in some one thing. Some in many! [*He unconsciously glances at himself in the mirror.*] All you've got to do is discover in *what!* Take me, for instance. [*He adjusts his tie at the mirror.*] My interest happens to lie in electro-dynamics. I'm taking a course in radio engineering at night school, Laura, on top of a fairly responsible job at the warehouse. I'm taking that course and studying public speaking.

*   *   *

Because I believe in the future of television! [*turning his back to her.*] I wish to be ready to go up right along with it. Therefore I'm planning to get in on the ground floor. In fact I've already made the right connections and all that remains is for the industry itself to get under way! Full steam— [*His eyes are starry.*] *Knowledge*—Zzzzzp! *Money*— Zzzzzp!—*Power!* That's the cycle democracy is built on!

[*His attitude is convincingly dynamic. He suddenly grins.*]

I guess you think I think a lot of myself!

SUMMERTREE

Ron Cowen

This is an unusual and touching play about a young soldier who is alone and dying in the jungle. He is leaning against a tree that reminds him of a tree from his childhood, and although he is hallucinating, he remembers with clarity his life, his parents, his girlfriend, and himself as a boy. All of these memories are scenes in the play. The following monologue opens the play with him slouched on the ground. For the young actor, there are several other monologues in this play.

◆

ACT I

The scene is a deep, green glen. At back center is the large, gnarled, heavy trunk of a tree. It rises into branches which spread out. A couple of geraniums are planted at the base of the tree.

The house and stage lights go to black. The Young Man takes his place, seated at the base of the tree, while the stage is dark.

A machine gun blast breaks the silence, followed quickly by a dim, broken, blue light pattern on the stage floor. At this moment the Girl appears down stage right, carrying a portable tape recorder, which is playing a Bach fugue. She crosses the stage from down right to down left and continues to off-stage up left, with the fugue still playing. As she crosses down stage center, the Soldier enters up stage left, runs to stage right, where he crouches a moment, then exits down stage right. As he crouches, the Boy enters up stage right, runs to stage center, looks right and left and then exits above the tree. As he goes out, a red glow rises on the Young Man, who begins first line of play. The fugue fades out on the line "Mom" in the first speech.

YOUNG MAN.
It's hot out here, just sitting and waiting. Shirt's sticking to my back. I hate it like this, wiping sweat out of my eyes. Damn. I'll just lie here and let the breeze cool my face. Ah. Just close my eyes and put my head back. I have to remember all these things. Hey, you're tickling me . . . ow! That hurts! Mom . . . Dad . . . ? I wish you could feel the palm of my hand. Can you see how smooth it is? Can you tell that it is warm? There are all these lines. All these little lines going all over, criss-crossing, entwining, stopping, then starting up again. (*He smiles, up.*) You know, hands are like leaves. (*Embarrassed at being obvious.*) But you know that. (*He picks up a leaf.*) Ever peel a leaf? You know. You peel off the skin or the flesh . . . the green part . . . and try and just leave the veins without breaking any of them. (*Peeling the leaf.*) Like this. (*To himself.*) Very slowly. Very carefully. (*Holds up his partly peeled leaf.*) You must do it very slowly and be

very cautious not to break a vein in two. See? It looks like a winter tree. Then you hold it up to the sun and see how it makes a shadow. It looks like a big skeleton's hand. (*He smiles, up.*) Did you ever wonder if a hand could be stripped like a leaf? (*Looks up.*) It could, you know. Sure. You very slowly, very carefully peel the skin away, being careful not to break anything. Then you hold the skeleton hand up to the light and see how it makes a shadow like a big, winter tree. If you care to try it yourself, I guarantee you, you won't feel a thing. Except yourself . . . screaming. You know, this tree has been here for years and years. It's funny. The first thing I wanted to do when I was a kid, was to dig it up and see it fall over. I guess all kids do.

EAT YOUR HEART OUT

Nick Hall

This is a humorous play that takes place in a Manhattan restaurant. Charlie is a personable and attractive young waiter who wants to be an actor. Between comical scenes with customers, he comes downstage and talks directly to the audience. The following monologue opens the play.

◆—◆—◆

CHARLIE.
If there's one thing I can't stand in the theatre, it's walking out alone on stage at the beginning of the evening to open a show cold. (*Grins.*) *But* it's better than waiting tables. I'm Charlie, (*Ironic.*) . . . your waiter for the evening. I'd rather be onstage tonight. Waiting tables is a toy job. You probably don't know what a toy job is. I'll explain. A toy job is a job that you don't really care about, that you do to make a living, while you wait for the chance to do the job you want to do. (*Beat. He measures the audience.*) But maybe you know already. Being a waiter is sort of a standard job for an actor; it's expected. I mean, if you're a dentist or an insurance salesman and someone says

130

"where're ya' workin' nowadays?," and you say, "I'm a waiter at this little French place on fifty-sixth street," they think you're a failure. But if you're an actor, they understand. So. (*Indicates the restaurant with a gesture.*) *Ici, personne ne parle francais.* (*Beat.*) That's the name of the place. (*Beat.*) Yeah, well I didn't get it the first time either. It means no one here speaks French. It's really a lunch place. At lunch they use four waiters. After lunch through dinner: one waiter. (*Indicates himself.*) We just get a few semi-regulars in the evening, and now, between lunch and dinner, nothing. (*By now* CHARLIE *has started to fiddle with things on the tables. Straightening.*) The food's good, French, reasonable. At lunch you can get a great meal here for about three-fifty, four bucks. Of course, the price soars if you start ordering little extras, like coffee. (*The* GIRL *enters.*) She's gotta be kidding. It's mid-afternoon. (*He checks his watch.*) Three-thirty. (*To the* GIRL.) Bonjour, m'mselle.

EAT YOUR HEART OUT

Nick Hall

•◆•

Charlie has just witnessed an argument between a man and a woman sitting at one of his tables. After they exit, he speaks to the audience. For more background on this play, see the previous introduction on page 130.

•◆•

CHARLIE.
See that? That's one of the problems with being a waiter. You hear snatches, fragments, and just as it's beginning to get interesting, they ask for the check. I always wanna know what happened. That's why I'd rather be in the theatre. First of all, in the theatre they would stay at home in their living room. On Friday night, they'd have a fight—Act One. On Saturday they'd have a complication—Act Two. And for a nice Act Three on Sunday morning, *they'd* make up and we'd all go home. That's the way it's supposed to be. (*Beat.*) Actually, in this particular case, I'll probably find out. I mean, they're regulars; they eat out all the time. He eats lunch out too. I'll probably run into him soon. They wanted eggs. Maybe

I should've suggested they stay here. We serve eggs. We serve Eggs Benedict and a mushroom omelet. (*During the above,* CHARLIE *has stacked the two glasses and the three candles onto his tray. He has also bundled up the tablecloths. He retires to the service area with them. He returns with three more tablecloths. The cloths are very noticeable, possibly a loud black and white pattern. He spreads them.*) I'm up for a Colgate commercial. We tested today. That means I got to spend half the day standing around in a towel, smiling. I didn't mind. Standing around in a towel, smiling is one of the things I do very, very well. Everybody said so. (*Smiles.*) That's my standing-around-in-a-towel-smiling smile. I've got a good chance. They liked me; I could tell. It all depends on whether they decide they want a smooth chest or a hairy chest. So. (*The word "So" used by* CHARLIE *is generally a verbal shrug.*) I wish they'd let me know. I phoned my agent. She was out. At least they said she was out. Maybe she was. I checked my service this evening. Seven times. Finally they said, "Charlie, don't call again. If anything happens, we'll get to you." But I don't trust 'em. I'll call again. (*As soon as he had spread the cloths,* CHARLIE, *while talking, took off his apron and tie. Now, carrying them, he retires to the service area. He returns immediately carrying a tray on which there are three town-crier style handbells. There is also a cummerbund and a large bow tie on the tray. Both are made of the same fabric as the tablecloths. There are menus on the tray.* CHARLIE *sets a bell out on each table.*) A brand new restaurant on Third Avenue in the twenties. Just opened two days ago. Now I don't want to make you nervous, but three waiters have quit already. I'm just filling in for a day

or two. (*Rings a bell.*) Cute, hunh? For service.
It's called Tintintabulation. There's a dead raven
on the cash register. (*Picking up the cummerbund
and bow tie and putting them on, not pleased with
the cutesy color coordination.*) I've been changing
restaurants so much lately, sometimes I forget
where I'm supposed to be. I should settle down,
I guess. Well, I will soon. There's a time limit set
on my acting career. Two years. Self-imposed.
When I started out I said, two years and that's it.
Not a day more. Either I make it in two years or
finis. That was four years ago. Nearly five. So. It's
not that I'm really hungry to be rich or famous
or anything. I mean, it'd be nice, but I wanna be
an actor. Just a good, working actor. That's all.
The money and everything isn't all that important. Just working at my craft, because working
at your craft is why I really want to be a movie star. A superstar. I wanna taste that. I wanna
bite into it and let the juice run down my face.
(*The vehemence with which* CHARLIE *ends this speech
is probably as surprising to* CHARLIE *as it is to us.
In any case, it has prevented* CHARLIE *from noticing
that the* BOY *has entered toward the end of the speech
and is waiting, irritated, to be seated.* CHARLIE
"comes out of it" and registers the BOY.*) Oh, hi!
Sorry, I didn't see you there.

LILIOM

Ferenc Molnár

The Rodgers and Hammerstein musical, *Carousel*, is based on this play. Liliom is a carousel barker who is considered a ne'er-do-well in his European community. However, a young girl, Julie, has fallen in love with him and is pregnant with his child. In the following scene, Liliom is on a stretcher, dying. Julie's lines, which mainly consist of "yes," are deleted and marked by asterisks. She is holding his hand while he tries to explain his love for her.

•◆•

LILIOM.
[*Raises himself with difficulty; speaks lightly at first, but later soberly, defiantly.*] Little—Julie—there's something—I want to tell you—like when you go to a restaurant—and you've finished eating—and it's time—to pay—then you can have to count up everything—everything you owe—well—I beat you—not because I was mad at you—no—only because I can't bear to see anyone crying. You always cried—on my account—and, well, you see,—I never learned a trade—what kind of a caretaker would I make? But anyhow—I wasn't

going back to the carousel to fool with the girls.
No, I spit on them all—understand?

*   *   *

And—as for Hollinger—he's good enough—Mrs.
Muskat can get along all right with him. The
jokes he tells are mine—and the people laugh
when he tells them—but I don't care.—I didn't
give you anything—no home—not even the food
you ate—but you don't understand.—It's true
I'm not much good—but I couldn't be a caretaker—and so I thought maybe it would be better
over there—in America—do you see?

*   *   *

I'm not asking—forgiveness—I don't do that—I
don't. Tell the baby—if you like.

*   *   *

Tell the baby—I wasn't much good—but tell
him—if you ever talk about me—tell him—I
thought—perhaps—over in America—but that's
no affair of yours. [*Pause.*] I'm not asking forgiveness. For my part the police can come now.—If
it's a boy—if it's a girl.—Perhaps I'll see the Lord
God today.—Do you think I'll see Him?

*   *   *

I'm not afraid—of the police Up There—if they'll
only let me come up in front of the Lord God Himself—not like down here where an officer stops
you at the door. If the carpenter asks you—yes—

be his wife—marry him. And the child—tell him he's his father.—He'll believe you—won't he?

* * *

When I beat you—I was right.—You mustn't always think—you mustn't always be right.—Liliom can be right once, too.—It's all the same to me who was right.—It's so dumb. Nobody's right—but they all think they are right.—A lot they know!

* * *

Julie—come—hold my hand tight.

* * *

Tighter, still tighter—I'm going—[*Pauses.*] Julie—

OH DAD, POOR DAD, MAMMA'S HUNG YOU IN THE CLOSET AND I'M FEELING SO SAD

Arthur L. Kopit

This play is described as a farce in its three scenes. But it has sad undertones for the young man, Jonathan, who is pathetically insecure and completely under his bizarre mother's domination. He has been locked up in a lavish suite in a Caribbean hotel by his mother. But Rosalie, the resourceful and attractive young baby-sitter, has gotten the key and let herself in to visit him. Jonathan is terrified but definitely interested in her. He speaks with a bad stutter, which is a challenge to a young actor; he should be careful about exaggerating it or making it too blatantly comic. One short line by Rosalie is deleted and marked by asterisks.

●◆●

JONATHAN.
Well, I made it out of lenses and tubing. The lenses I had because Ma-Ma-Mother gave me a set of lenses so I could see my stamps better. I have a fabulous collection of stamps, as well as a fantastic collection of coins and a simply unbelievable collection of books. Well, sir, Ma-Ma-Mother gave me these lenses so I

could see my stamps better. She suspected that some were fake so she gave me the lenses so I might be—able to see. You see? Well, sir, I happen to have nearly a billion sta-stamps. So far I've looked closely at 1,352,769. I've discovered three actual fakes! Number 1,352,767 was a fake. Number 1,352,768 was a fake, and number 1,352,769 was a fake. They were stuck together. Ma-Mother made me feed them immediately to her flytraps. Well—(*He whispers.*) one day, when Mother wasn't looking—that is, when she was out, I heard an airplane flying. An airplane—somewhere—far away. It wasn't very loud, but still I heard it. An airplane. Flying—somewhere, far away. And I ran outside to the porch so that I might see what it looked like. The airplane. With hundreds of people inside it. Hundreds and hundreds and hundreds of people. And I thought to myself, if I could just see—if I could just see what they looked like, the people, sitting at their windows, looking out—and flying. If I could see—*just* once—if I could see *just once* what they looked like—then I might—know what I—what I . . . (*Slight pause.*) So I—built a telescope in case the plane ever—came back again. The tubing came from an old blowgun. (*He reaches behind the bureau and produces a huge blowgun, easily a foot larger than he.*) Mother brought it back from her last hunting trip to Zanzibar. The lenses were the lenses she had given me for my stamps. So I built it. My telescope. A telescope so I might be able to see. And—(*He walks out to the porch.*) and—and I *could see*! I could! I COULD! I really could. For miles and miles I could see. For miles and miles and *miles!* (*He begins to lift it up to look through but stops, for some reason, before he's brought it up to his eye.*) Only . . .

       *   *   *

(*Sadly.*) I know. That's the trouble. You take the time to build a telescope that can sa-see for miles, then there's nothing out there to see. Ma-Mother says it's a Lesson in Life.

OH DAD, POOR DAD, MAMMA'S HUNG YOU IN THE CLOSET AND I'M FEELING SO SAD

Arthur L. Kopit

This second monologue by Jonathan almost immediately follows his previous one. There has been a short intervening dialogue between Jonathan and Rosalie. For more information about this play, see the previous introductionon page 138.

•—◆—•

JONATHAN.
I—I don't—know. I don't know why. I mean. I've—nnnnnnnnever really thought—about going out. I—guess it's—just natural for me to—stay inside. (*He laughs nervously as if that explained everything.*) You see—I've got so much to do. I mean, all my sssssstamps and—ca-coins and books. The pa-pa-plane might fffffffly overhead while I was was going downstairs. And then thhhhere are—the plants ta-to feeeeeeed. And I enjoy vvvery much wa—watching you and all yyyyyyour chil-dren. I've—really got so ma-many things—to—do. Like—like my future, for instance. Ma-Mother says I'm going to be great. That's—that's—that's what she—says. I'm going to be great. I sssswear. Of course, she doesn't

141

know ex-actly what I'm—going to be great in—
so she sits every afternoon for—for two hours
and thinks about it. Na-na-naturally I've—got to
be here when she's thinking in case she—thinks
of the answer. Otherwise she might forget and
I'd never know—what I'm ga-going to be great
in. You—see what I mean? I mean, I've—I've
gggggot so many things to do I—just couldn't
possibly get anything done if I ever—went—
outside. (*There is a silence.* JONATHAN *stares at*
ROSALIE *as if he were hoping that might answer
her question sufficiently.*) Besides, Mother locks the
front door.

SLOW DANCE ON
THE KILLING GROUND

William Hanley

This moving and interesting three-character play takes place in a small store in a district of warehouses and factories in Brooklyn. It is the only lit place in the darkness. Two frightened young people arrive there separately, and they and the storekeeper, Glas, talk through the night right up to the climax of the play. Randall, a young black man of eighteen, "slim, wiry, handsome" and dressed rather oddly in an Edwardian cape, enters at the opening of the play. He is breathless and apparently very agitated. In the following monologue, he talks to Glas about his life.

●◆●

RANDALL.
(*Turns, crosses R. to counter. Puts down hat and umbrella. Leans toward Glas.*) True, all true. Truly. Actually it's the only thing in my life for which I have an explanation, the hole in my heart. (*Turns L. Takes off glasses.*) Randall, you see, was conceived of a union between his mother and one of the numberless men she never saw again, his

143

mother being a prostitute by profession. Conceived of lust and the natural hungers of the flesh, but without love. It was that absence of love that left the hole in Randall's heart, no mistake. I mean, (*Turns back to Glas. Takes off cape, puts it on counter.*) picture, if you will, Randall, at the age of approximately six months when his momma discovered that (D. *to above stool.*) his heart hadn't healed up all the way, like it was supposed to, like everyone else's, while he was still in his momma's womb. A comparatively rare occurrence, indeed. So they executed with great skill and care a delicate operation and sewed up that nasty hole in Randall's wee heart. A colloquial expression, that, a hole in the heart, but true. True. She used it often, his momma did. It got so that Randall began to think if he heard that expression one more time he be about ready to cut somebody's throat, it being a toss-up whether it would be his own or his momma's. (*Sits stool* D.R., *starts to rock.*) He was saved from the perpetration of that rash act, however, by the fact that about that time his momma was apprehended for offerin' her charms to an officer of the law. Funny thing is he didn't arrest her until after he'd accepted her offer. Know what I mean? Reason I know is, I was in the closet at the time, watchin', unbeknownst to momma and her gentleman visitor who proved subsequently to be an officer of the law. (*Stops rocks, turns* D.) I was seven years old at the time, and fond of playin' in momma's closet. Poor momma. That old cop gettin' up offa her and pullin' up his pants and flashin' his shiny old badge, was she surprised. Mad too, of course, but mostly surprised, I remember that very clear. That was her third arrest for lewd and lascivious behavior and (*Off stool. Crosses to above table. Faces* D.L.) she got detained for ninety days in the Women's House of Detention. It was durin' that time of her detention that somebody or other took high offense at the fact of me striking one of my playmates lightly on the face without first taking the precaution of removing the beer can opener from my hand, an oversight which made for quite a little bit of a mess so far as the little chap's face was concerned. (*Looks at Glas. Crosses* R. *to* D.C. *facing* D.R.) So, my momma bein' elsewhere occupied and me bein' otherwise kinless, they up and put me in a kinda (*Turns* D.) *home.* That's where they first discovered about me bein' so smart and all 'cause at the time I was carryin' in my pocket a book of poems which I had acquired free of charge under somewhat surreptitious circumstances and which had been authored by someone whose name I couldn't pronounce and they said what was I doin' with that book, a book like that, and I said readin' it. (*Crosses* U.R. *to ladder looking into hallway.*) Then after a while, they let me go back to my momma who was free and swingin' again. Now you have a kinda montage effect showin' momma plyin' her trade and Randall gettin' the picture very gradual but very clear and this goes on for several years, Randall listenin' to the men clompin' up the stairs with his momma and down again alone, leavin' momma in the bedroom with the sound of running water. (*Turns* L. *and leans toward Glas.*) About that time was when she stopped usin' that expression. You know: about the hole in Randall's heart? She stopped usin' it and Randall started. Had a nice ring to it, that expression, and it explained a lotta things just right. Like for instance, the time (*Moves* D. *to bench.*) Randall is in the process of fleein' the scene of a crime, as they say, when a thirty-eight caliber bullet fired from the gun bein' held steadily in the hand of one of New York's Finest, marksmen all, when that bullet entered his back just under the left shoulder blade (*Slumps as imaginary bullet hits.*) and lodged against the back side of a rib, the force of the blow propelling Randall some ten feet or so right into the gutter on his face. And there Randall lay with his mouth in a little river of rainwater, shot through the heart. (*Turns to Glas.*) Oh, you know what the doctors said, naturally they said that bullet had struck him just an inch *below* the heart but he knew better, Randall did. He knew goddamned well that little old bullet had passed right through the hole in his heart and out the other side. (*Crosses L. sits on end of bench facing D.L.*) Follows two years of restitution for Randall in a woodsy little correctional farm for Youthful Offenders in the upper reaches of New York State. And wouldn't you know that on attainin' his freedom, who should be standin' there to greet him at the train station but his dear little momma? His momma who wrote him three letters in two years and never did manage to make him a visit in the flesh. (*Turns head D.*) But there she is, standin' in a silky green dress and a white hat, sayin' welcome home, Randall, you lookin' just fine. And Randall just look at her right in the eye for about a minute or two and says real quiet, go away, momma. Which disturbs her no end, for some reason or other and sets her to screaming on a graduated scale of pitch and intensity, following Randall across the marble vastness of the Grand Central Station and all the folks lookin' on and listenin' to the flashy, colored lady makin' all that racket, they're so uninhibited and spontaneous, those people. Her screamin' I'm your momma, Randall, I'm your momma no matter what, and various and assorted other demands of endearment. And the last thing Randall hears before he hit the top of the stairs, leavin' his mother puffin' at the bottom the last he hears was her screamin', you got no love in you! Which was all too true, of course. Because that piece which had never grown into Randall's heart? . . . That was the place where love is. Of course. (*Glas rises turns* U. *leans on counter. Pause. Randall turns to Glas.*) Never make a long story short, that's my motto. (*Stands, moves* U. *to between stools. Pause.*) Is your silence a profound one, Mister Glas? (*Randall picks up his hat. Randall speaks again in the dialect.*) Well, silence also speaks, daddy. (*Sings quietly. Puts on his glasses and cape. Picks up his umbrella.*) I went to the rock to hide my face, the rock cried out, no hiding place . . .

"MASTER HAROLD" . . .
AND THE BOYS

Athol Fugard

Hally is a seventeen-year-old white boy in South Africa in 1950 who is close to two black men— when apartheid was still legal. The play explores the tensions, the loneliness, and the changes in a young man's mind as he struggles with the status quo of his country and his own ambivalent feelings about race. The play takes place in a tea room where the two black men work. In this scene, Hally has come from school looking for the friendship and companionship of Sam and Willie.

●◆●

HALLY.
Which meant I got another rowing for hanging around the "servant's quarters." I think I spent more time in there with you chaps than anywhere else in that dump. And do you blame me? Nothing but bloody misery wherever you went. Somebody was always complaining about the food or my mother was having a fight with Micky Nash because she'd caught her with a petty officer in her room. Maud Meiring was another one. Remember those two? They were

prostitutes, you know. Soldiers and sailors from
the troopships. Bottom fell out of the business
when the war ended. God, the flotsam and jetsam
that life washed up on our shores! No joking, if it
wasn't for your room I would have been the first
certified ten-year-old in medical history. Ja, the
memories are coming back now. Walking home
from school and thinking: What can I do this
afternoon? Try out a few ideas but sooner or
later I'd end up in there with you fellows. I
bet you I could still find my way to your room
with my eyes closed. (*He does exactly that.*) Down
the corridor . . . telephone on the right which my
mom keeps locked because somebody is using
it on the sly and not paying . . . past the kitchen
and unappetising cooking smells . . . around the
corner into the backyard, hold my breath again
because there are more smells coming when I
pass your lavatory, then into that little passage-
way, first door on the right and into your room.
How's that?

"MASTER HAROLD" ...
AND THE BOYS

Athol Fugard

Hally is remembering with pleasure an afternoon
he spent with Sam. For more about this play, see
the previous introduction on page 148.

◆

HALLY.
It started off looking like another of those useless, nothing-to-do afternoons. I'd already been
down to Main Street looking for adventure, but
nothing had happened. I didn't feel like climb-
ing trees in the Donkin park, or pretending I
was a private eye and following a stranger ...
so, as usual: See what's cooking in Sam's room.
This time it was you on the floor. You had two
thin pieces of wood and you were smoothing
them down with a knife. It didn't look particularly interesting, but when I asked you what
you were doing, you just said, "Wait and see,
Hally. Wait ... and see." ... in that secret sort
of way of yours, so I knew there was a surprise coming. You teased me, you bugger, by
being deliberately slow and not answering my
questions!

(SAM *laughs*)

And whistling while you worked away! God, it was infuriating! I could have brained you! It was only when you tied them together in a cross and put that down on the brown paper that I realized what you were doing. Sam is making a kite! And when I asked you, you said: Yes . . . ! (*shaking his head with disbelief*) The sheer audacity of it took my breath away. I mean seriously, what the hell does a black man know about flying a kite? I'll be honest with you, Sam, I had no hopes for it. If you think I was excited and happy, you got another guess coming. In fact I was shit-scared that we were going to make fools of ourselves. When we left the boarding house to go up onto the hill, I was praying quietly that there wouldn't be any other kids around to laugh at us.

"MASTER HAROLD" . . . AND THE BOYS

Athol Fugard

In the following monologue, Hally speaks to his mother on the telephone, and the anguish and conflicts that rage inside him become apparent. These emotions add to the challenge for the young actor because he must listen and respond to someone whom the audience does not hear. For more background on this play, see the introduction on page 148.

◆

HALLY.

(*to the telephone*) Hello, Mom . . . No, everything is okay here. Just doing my homework . . . What's your news? . . . You've what? . . . (*Pause. He takes the receiver away from his ear for a few seconds, then goes back to it.*) Yes, I'm still here. Oh well, I give up now. Why did you do it, Mom? . . . Well I just hope you know what you've let us in for . . . (*loudly*) I said I hope you know what you've let us in for! It's the end of the peace and quiet we've been having. (*softly*) Where is he? (*normal voice*) He can't hear us from in there. But for God's sake, Mom, what happened? I told you to be firm with him . . . Then you and the nurses should have held him down, taken his crutches away . . . I know only too well he's my father! . . . I'm not being disrespectful but I'm sick and tired of emptying stinking chamber pots full of plegm and piss . . . Yes I do! When you're not there he asks me to do it . . . If you really want to know the truth, that's why I've got no appetite for my food . . . Yes! There's a lot of things you don't know about. For your information, I still haven't got that science textbook I need. And you know why? He borrowed the money you gave me for it . . . Because I didn't want to start another fight between you two . . . He says that everytime . . . Alright, Mom! (*viciously*) Then just remember to start hiding your bag away again because he'll be at your purse before long for money for booze. And when he's well enough to come down here, you better keep an eye on the till as well, because that is also going to develop a leak . . . Then don't complain to me when he starts his old tricks . . . Yes, you do. I get it from you on one side and from him on the other, and it makes life hell for me. I'm not going to be the peace-maker anymore. I'm warning you now; when the two of you start fighting again, I'm leaving home . . . Mom, if you start crying I'm going to put down the receiver . . . Okay . . . (*lowering his voice to a vicious whisper*) Okay, Mom. I heard you. (*desperate*) No. Because I don't want to. I'll see him when I get home! Mom! . . . (*Pause. When he speaks again his tone changes completely. It is not simply pretense. We sense a genuine emotional conflict.*) Welcome home chum! . . . What's that? . . . Don't be silly, Dad. You being home is just about the best news in the world . . . I bet you are. Bloody depressing there with everybody going on about their ailments, hey! . . . How you feeling? . . . Good . . . Here as well, pal. Coming down cats and dogs . . . (*a weak little laugh*) That's right. Just the day for a kip and a toss in your old Uncle Ned . . . Everything's just hunky-dory on my side Dad . . . Well to start with, there's a nice pile of comics for you on the counter . . . Yes, old Kemple brought them in. Batman and Robin, Submariner . . . just your cup of tea . . . I will . . . Yes, we'll spin a few yarns tonight . . . Okay chum, see you in a little while . . . No, I promise. I'll come straight home . . . (*Pause. His mother comes back on the phone.*) Mom? Okay. I'll lock up now . . . What? . . . Oh, the brandy . . . Yes, I'll remember! . . . I'll put it in my suitcase now, for God's sake. I know well enough what will happen if he doesn't get it. I was kind to him, Mom. I didn't say anything nasty! . . . Alright. Bye. (*End of telephone conversation. A desolate* HALLY *doesn't move. A strained silence.*)

TAKE A GIANT STEP

Louis Peterson

This play is about the only black family living on a middle-class street in a 1950s New England town. The action revolves around seventeen-year-old Spence, who is going through the usual throes of youth as well as being caught between his black pride and an insensitive white world. This is before the 1960s' advent of civil rights and the understanding of black pride. Spence has been raised to be deferential and polite to white people. In the following scene, Spence talks to his grandmother, the only person who seems to understand what pride is and why it is necessary. Her lines have been deleted and marked by asterisks as Spence describes what happened to him in school that day.

●-◆-●

SPENCE.
(*Pause.*) Well—from the very beginning of school I could've told you that that Miss Crowley and I weren't going to see eye to eye.

* * *

155

The history teacher, Gram. The one that thinks she's cute. She's always giving the guys a preview of the latest fashions in underwear.

*   *   *

That's the one. Well, today they started talking about the Civil War and one of the smart little skirts at the back of the room wanted to know why the Negroes in the South didn't rebel against slavery. Why did they wait for the Northerners to come down and help them? And this Miss Crowley went on to explain how they were stupid and didn't have sense enough to help themselves. (*Crosses chair Left of table; sits.*) Well, anyway, Gram, when she got through talking they sounded like the worst morons that ever lived and I began to wonder how they'd managed to live a few thousand years all by themselves in Africa with nobody's help. I would have let it pass—see—except that the whole class was whispering and giggling and turning around and looking at me—so I got up and just stood next to my desk looking at her. She looked at me for a couple of minutes and asked me if perhaps I had something to say in the discussion. I said I might have a lot of things to say if I didn't have to say them in the company of such dumb jerks. Then I asked her frankly what college she went to.

*   *   *

She told me I was being impudent. I told her it was not my intention to be impudent but I would

honestly like to know. So she puts one hand on
her hip—kinda throwing the other hip out of joint
at the same time—and like she wants to spit on
me she says "Scoville." Then I says, "And they
didn't teach you nothing about the *up*rising of
the slaves during the Civil War—or Frederick
Douglas?" She says, "No—they didn't." "In that
case," I said, "I don't want to be in your crummy
history class." And I walk out of the room. When
I get out in the hall, Gram, I'm shaking, I'm so
mad—and I had this cigar I was going to sell for
a sundae. I knew I couldn't eat a sundae now
'cause it would just make me sick so—I just had
to do something so I went into the Men's Room
and smoked the cigar. I just had about two drags
on the thing when in comes the janitor and hauls
me down to old Hasbrook's office—and when I
get down there—there's Miss Crowley and old
Hasbrook talking me over in low tones—and
in five short minutes he'd thrown me out of
school.

THE CHERRY ORCHARD

Anton Chekhov

This gentle but profound play deals with the social and political changes occurring in Russia in 1904, but its message is human and universal. A crass, businessman, the son of a former serf, is buying the estate and treasured cherry orchard of the impoverished but genteel landowner, Madame Ranevskaya. In spite of the melancholy hanging over everyone, Trofimoff, a student, remains idealistic and hopeful. In the following scene, he talks to Anya, the seventeen-year-old daughter of Madame Ranevskaya. Several lines are deleted and marked by asterisks.

•◆•

TROFIMOFF.

All Russia is our orchard. The earth is immense and beautiful, and on it are many wonderful places. (*A pause*) Just think, Anya: your grandfather, great-grandfather and all your ancestors were slave owners, in possession of living souls, and can you doubt that from every cherry in the orchard, from every leaf, from every trunk, human beings are looking at you, can it be that you don't hear their voices? To possess living souls, well, that depraved all of you who lived before and who are living now, so that your mother and you, and your uncle no longer notice that you live by debt, at somebody else's expense, at the expense of those very people whom you wouldn't let past your front door—We are at least two hundred years behind the times, we have as yet absolutely nothing, we have no definite attitude toward the past, we only philosophize, complain of our sadness or drink vodka. Why, it is quite clear that to begin to live in the present we must first atone for our past, must be done with it; and we can atone for it only through suffering, only through uncommon, incessant labor. Understand that, Anya.

*   *   *

If you have the household keys, throw them in the well and go away. Be free as the wind.

*   *   *

Believe me, Anya, believe me! I am not thirty yet, I am young, I am still a student, but I have already borne so much! Every winter I am hungry, sick, anxious, poor as a beggar, and—where has destiny not chased me, where haven't I been! And yet, my soul has always, every minute, day and night, been full of inexplicable premonitions. I have a premonition of happiness, Anya, I see it already—

*   *   *

Yes, the moon is rising. (*A pause*) Here is happiness, here it comes, comes always nearer and nearer, I hear its footsteps now. And if we shall not see it, shall not come to know it, what does that matter? Others will see it!

BUTTERFLIES ARE FREE

Leonard Gershe

•—•

This monologue opens the play. Don, in his early twenties and "lean and good-looking" with neatly combed hair, is listening to a tape when the phone rings. He is from Scarsdale, New York, and trying to make it on his own in an apartment in New York City. This is quite a challenge because Don is blind. The playwright describes Don talking on the phone "in a tone indicating he has said this hundreds of times."

•—•

DON.
(*Speaking to ringing phone—after second ring.*) I'm fine, thank you. How are you? (*Crosses above director's chair to sofa and turns off recorder.*) It's warm here. How is it in Scarsdale? (*Crosses to sink, puts glass in it.*) Well, it's warm here, too. (*Crosses and picks up the phone.*) Hello, Mother. . . . I just knew. When you call the phone doesn't ring. It just says "m" is for the million things she gave you. I'm fine, thank you. How are you? . . . (*Sits sofa.*) It's warm here. How is it in Scarsdale? Well, it's warm here, too. The apartment is great.

I love it. Last night? I didn't do anything last night. I mean I didn't go out. I had some friends in—a little party. . . . I don't know how many people were here. Do you have to have a number? Twelve and a half, how's that? . . . No, they didn't stay too late. . . . When? (*Rises, picks up phone, crosses with it onto platform to behind D. end of dining table.*) No! No, not this afternoon. . . . I don't care. Come to town and go to Saks, but you're not coming down here. Because we agreed to two months, didn't we? (*Suddenly the noise of a conversational TV program is heard blaring in the next apartment.*) What? . . . No, I didn't turn on my radio. It's coming from next door. . . . I don't know . . . a girl. . . . She just moved in a couple of days ago . . . I don't know her name. I haven't met her. . . . It's her radio . . . Don't worry, it won't go on. . . . Yes, I'll tell her. . . . No, I don't want you to tell her. Just go to Saks and go home. . . . I can hardly hear you. We'll talk tomorrow. Goodbye. (DON *hangs up, crosses L. to the door that connects the apartment and raps, angrily.*) Hey, would you please . . . (*Knocking louder and shouting*) Would you mind lowering your radio? (*TV program is turned off.*)

NOURISH THE BEAST

Steve Tesich

A drama filled with wonderfully comic characters, this play is about a family struggling to survive as a family. The following scene, with Bruno talking to his not-quite sister, Sylvia, and someone called Criminal, reflects the sad, funny lines of the play. They are sitting at a kitchen table in a modest apartment. Short lines by other characters are deleted and marked by asterisks as Bruno talks about his childhood.

●—◆—●

BRUNO.
Let me continue . . . I don't know how old I was when they put in the orphanage . . . not very . . . and the first time I heard the word "orphan" I thought it was this guy's name. Billy Orphan. Then I found out that I was an orphan too, and I figured that Billy and I were related. Then I found out that we were all orphans . . . and I figured . . . hell . . . somebody must be lying . . . we can't all be relatives.

*   *   *

Let me finish. So we were all orphans but I still didn't know what the word meant except that we talked about everything in terms of that one word . . . the outside world was a non-orphanage . . . those that got placed were de-orphanated . . . those that came back were re-orphanated. For a long time I thought only boys were orphans . . . so when I grew up I wanted to be a girl. Then I found out that there were female orphans too . . . we called them orphenes. But I still didn't know what the word meant. So I asked one of the guards one day . . . what's an orphan? He said it was somebody that nobody liked. But these other orphans liked me . . . Billy liked me . . . so I asked him if that made me a non-orphan. He said no . . . He said being liked by another orphan didn't count.

*   *   *

So I started thinking that nothing that happened in the orphanage counted. The only things that mattered happened on the outside. For the whole time that that I was there some police athletic league kept promising to take us to a ball game. We went to bed every night hoping that tomorrow was the big day when we'd go to a ball game. Hell, we didn't know what a ball game was . . . properly speaking . . . but it was on the outside so we assumed it was something incredible . . . something unheard of . . . and finally the big day came and this man took us all to a ball game.

*   *   *

The Yankees won.

*   *   *

That was it. The Yankees won . . . And all of us orphans sat there scratching our ass thinking . . . You mean this is it . . . this is the real thing . . . That's why I still go to ball games . . . I figure one of these days I'm going to see it the way I thought it would be . . . you know . . . the ball game of the century . . . the ball game of all time . . .

*   *   *

And you know what? . . . when I go there I see some of those orphans I once knew . . . Billy's there every time . . . They're all grown up and everything but still looking orphany as hell . . . still waiting for the ball game . . . you see don't you . . . you see how we were tricked into thinking that the outside world was so exciting and full of wonders . . . not that we thought it was all good . . . but we did think it was full of extremes . . . that's it . . . extremes. . . . the most beautiful and the ugliest things were on the outside . . . nothing in between . . . the orphanage was in between . . . and that's why I became a cop.

*   *   *

I thought that by being a cop I'd be able to find those extremes . . . and sometimes I think I'm close . . . Sometimes I'd be walking my beat and suddenly I hear this screaming . . . I mean screaming so painful your heart wants to commit suicide . . . and I think to myself . . . Hot dog! This is it! This is the saddest goddamned thing that ever happened in the world! And I rush to the house . . . I rush upstairs and what do I find . . . This old lady's screaming because her parakeet ate something foul and was vomiting all over the cage.

*   *   *

Swear to God, Sylvie . . . that damned parakeet was barfing like a truck driver . . . the old lady screaming her head off . . . for some reason she turned a fan on it . . . there it was . . . birdbarf all over the wallpaper . . .

CALL ME BY MY RIGHTFUL NAME

Michael Shurtleff

This interesting play examines a variety of relationships: family, man-woman, and race. Robert Duvall and Alvin Ailey played the original roommates, one white and one black, living in a converted loft while students at Columbia University.

Paul, the young African-American Columbia student has just arrived home after a short singing tour and is telling his roommate about a past relationship with a white woman. A few lines at the end of the scene are deleted and marked by asterisks to make a more effective ending for the monologue. For more about this play, see page 170.

◆━◆

PAUL.

(*Grinning, then serious.*) I've never told anyone what happened that night. A thing can get too important if you *hoard* it. Besides, it's time I told you things about me. Isn't it? (*Rises, crosses to corner platform* U. *Doug goes to bed, sits.*) It was a couple of months after I broke off with this girl I just told you about, my golden girl, the girl I loved the way the songs go. I was just knocking around after that and I didn't care much what happened. So one night about a month before I moved in here there was this doll, Inez, came into the club. She was with a crowd and she sent me a note asking me to come to sing for a party she was having. A cool fifty bucks enclosed. I thought, what the hell. A cool fifty. I thought what the hell about everything then, since I'd sent my golden girl away. (*Crosses D. to star.*) This Inez, she had the palest skin you ever saw, the kind you can almost see through, as if the veins were being x-rayed; and long black hair that made her skin look even whiter. (*Crosses U. to locker on platform.*) After I sang at her party, she came out to the elevator with me. She put her hand on mine; against mine, hers looked so white, almost impurely white. She wanted to know where to reach me, in case she heard of anyone else who wanted me to sing. Such a penthouse girl. (*Crosses R. of sofa to C.*) So in a few days she called me and I made a date with her, still what the hell. We started balling a lot after that. Inez made all the plans and that was okay with me. We'd meet in a bar or I'd stand on a street corner and wait for her to pick me up in that crazy foreign car of hers, all white, just like her—even the floor. (*Sits at desk chair.*) We went to a lot of parties, sometimes in penthouses and sometimes in basements where you sat on the floor and drank that stinkin' red wine and she'd use that white mink coat of hers for a rug. I never saw a white mink coat before, did you? She knew a hell of a lot of people, at least she was acquainted with them; I don't think we ever saw the same people twice. Or we'd sit in the back row at the movies and hold hands but that's the closest she'd let us come to being alone. She loved movies, any kind, hours of 'em. (*Crossing to stool.*) She'd never look at another guy; she always acted as if she belonged to me, no matter who we were with. I couldn't figure Inez out, but she was sure good for my ego. (*Crosses to U.R. platform.*) She made up her own world and she walked through it like a princess and I didn't have to think about mine. (*At stool again.*) And then one night—that night—I met her in a bar and we had a lot to drink and I asked her again if we couldn't be alone and finally she said she couldn't stand it any more and she wanted to take me to her place. So we went there and while I was fixing drinks, she wandered around looking at it—at her own all-white apartment—so carefully as if she were memorizing it—as if she were the stranger there and not me—and then I kissed her and she hung onto me like she always did, and I put my hand on her breast just like she always wanted me to, and I thought everything was going to be just fine. (*Paul finishes his glass and puts it down.*) All of a sudden, she jumped away from me like she'd been burned. She stood there and screamed at me, "You filthy nigger! Get your dirty black hands off of me." (*Crosses D. to star.*) She started to smash things, she threw a lamp through the window, screaming and hollering—all the filthy words you ever heard but mostly rape and nigger and black devil—stuff like that. When she smashed the window and began to holler for help, I realized what a spot she had me in, so I tore the hell out of there, down the back service stairs six at a time. I walked and walked—and—I ended up in that bar you work in.

CALL ME BY MY RIGHTFUL NAME

Michael Shurtleff

This monologue is by Doug and takes place on Christmas Eve. His brother, Elliot, has just left, disconsolate, because he has found his former girlfriend at Doug's apartment after she rejected him. One exclamation by the girlfriend is deleted and marked by asterisks.

•◆•

DOUG.

(*Doug rises, crosses up to* U. *post.*) Tell the folks I wish 'em—Merry Christmas. (*Crosses* D. *to* D.L. *chair.*) You don't know. It's not just Paul. It's not just this. It's not just Elliot. All that stuff about his girls. I saved him from marrying all them broads. Not one of 'em good enough for him.

* * *

(*Crosses* U. *of coffee table, picks up bottle, puts bottle and glass on desk, sits on milk box.*) Present company excepted, of course. Although, I must say you're the most treacherous one. Why didn't you tell me you walked out on Elliot tonight? Oh, it's

not just this. It's everything. Every god damned
thing I ever do—to Elliot, to my folks, to all
decent and law-abiding citizens. I start out with
the best of intentions—and look at it, it always
backfires. I always look like the guilty one. You
know why? Because I'm not noble and I don't
live by no made up rules. Because I do what
I feel, see? No one else does that. You know
why? They're afraid. I'm not afraid. They—they
try to make me look like I'm wrong. I'm not!
You know, that's the funny part of it, I'm not.
I'm honest. And honesty does not pay. It puts
you right behind the eight ball, because they all
want you to be hypocritical and namby pamby
and I refuse! God damn, I'm going to go right
on being who I am. I'm not like Elliot. Brave and
noble—and sneaking off home like a wounded
puppy, never uttering a sound. I'd howl! I'd let
'em know they couldn't steal my girl right out
from under my nose! Now, look, human beings
are supposed to talk. You know that? Nobody
talks any more. They sit around in dark haunchy
rooms looking at the pitchers on that obscene
lit'le box and there's no *communication*. They
don't know how—to reach out and *touch* each
other. Touch. They're all scared to death because
they don't know how to talk any more. Sex scares
'em. Thinkin' scares 'em. Bein' real scares 'em.
Mostly—touchin' scares 'em. (*Rises, picks up bottle and glass, crosses to her.*) I ain't gonna give in,
see: I'm gonna reach right out and grab hold of
people and talk to 'em and give 'em a good
shake and make 'em answer! That's what I'm
gonna do! Grab hold of things, that's what you
gotta do, grab hold of what you believe in and

hold on! (*Crosses* D.L. *of sofa.*) I am not goin' to have anything to do with you. Why didn't you tell me you left Elliot that note tonight? (*Puts bottle and glass on stool sits* D. *sofa.*)

IT'S CALLED
THE SUGAR PLUM

Israel Horovitz

This funny two-character, one-act play begins with the audience learning that Zuckerman, a twenty-two-year-old Harvard student, has accidentally run over and killed a young man on a skateboard. It would be a tragic scene except that in the playwright's hands, it becomes comic and satirical. The girlfriend of the victim confronts Zuckerman, and it becomes apparent that she is a superficial young woman enjoying the drama. After the short visit, the two begin their own intimate relationship. The following monologue is delivered by Zuckerman to the girlfriend, to Joanna.

◆

ZUCKERMAN.
That's right. Cellar door. Name two other words more beautiful. Go on, try. You just can't. Cellar door. (*He's excited again. Sits in bed* L. *of Joanna.*) Hey. You want to hear a great story? I mean a *great* story. It happened back home. I used to pass a gourmet shop on my way to Boston. When I came into my Uncle's to work on Sunday. I was just a kid then. I used to come in every Sunday

173

from Wakefield. On the bus. Anyway. There was this gourmet shop. German. They sold pastries and stuff to make your own pastries. Anyway. They had this terrific sign in their window for years advertising dough for strudel. Huge sign. Strudel dough. It was up for years. I used to pass it every Sunday. And I used to think about all those people who had to keep staring at it every day. They never ever changed the sign. I mean, it just *hung* there, taped to the window getting old and sort of yellow and terrible. Strudel dough. Get it? So one day, I got off the bus near the pastry shop; and I took a magic marker and right under "strudel dough" I wrote "strudel dee!!" Isn't that beautiful? (*He's laughing.*) Strudel dough. Strudel dee. Can you imagine what all those poor people said when they saw it? After all those years of passing that sign, all of a sudden it's funny. Strudel dough. Strudel dee. You think that's funny, don't you?

MOONCHILDREN

Michael Weller

This play, written in 1971, features a group of young students sharing a house during the trying times of the Vietnam War. The following monologue takes place on their last day in the house. It is time for graduation and everyone has left except for Bob, a musician who has difficulty expressing his feelings. He is talking to his former girlfriend, Kathy, who has returned to pick up her grades. She has just asked him, why he has not told his friends that his mother has died. A short line by Kathy has been deleted and marked by asterisks.

●◆●

BOB.

(*No emotion.*) Oh, I don't know. A little cunning. A little fortitude. A little perseverance. (*Pause.*) I couldn't believe it. Not the last time anyway. They put her in this room. I don't know what you call it. They bring everybody there just before they kick the bucket. They just sort of lie there looking at each other, wondering what the hell they got in common to talk about. I couldn't believe that anyone could look like she looked

175

and still be alive. (*Pause.*) She knew. I'm sure of
that. (*Pause.*) Once, I remember, she tried to tell
me something. I mean this noise came out of
somewhere around her mouth, like somebody
running a stick over a fence or something, and
I thought maybe she's trying to tell me something.
So I leaned over to hear better and I caught a whiff
of that breath. Like fried puke. And I was sick all
over her. (*Pause. Brighter.*) But you want to know
something funny, and I mean this really is funny, so you can laugh if you like. There was this
lady dying next to my mother and she kept talking about her daughter Susan. Well, Susan came
to visit the day I puked on Mom. And you know
what? It was only Susan Weinfeld which doesn't
mean anything to you but she happens to have
been the girl I spent a good many of my best
months as a sophomore in high school trying to
lay. In fact, her virginity almost cost me a B+ in
history and here we were, six years later, staring
at each other across two dying mothers. I want
to tell you something, Kathy. She looked fantastic. And I could tell she was thinking the same
thing about me. I mean that kind of scene doesn't
happen every day. It was like . . . (*Thinks.*) . . . it
was like how we were the first time. Maybe, just
possibly, a little better. So we went out and had
a coffee in Mr. Doughnut and started groping
each other like crazy under the counter and I
mean we just couldn't keep our hands off each
other so I suggested we get a cab down to my
mother's place since, you know, there happened
to be no one there at the moment. But the funniest thing was when we get down to Mom's place
and you know all those stairs you have to go up
and there's Susan all over me practically scream-

ing for it and I start fumbling around with the keys in the lock and none of them would fit. I must've tried every key about fifty fucking times and none of them would fit. Boy, what a drag. (*Pause.*) Oh, we got in all right. Finally. I had to go downstairs, through the Salvatore's apartment, out the window, up the fire escape and through Mom's place but when I opened the front door, guess what? There's poor old Susan asleep on the landing. She really looked cute. I hated to wake her up. Anyway, by the time we'd made coffee and talked and smoked about a million cigarettes each we didn't feel like it any more. Not really. We did it anyway but, you know, just to be polite, just to make some sense out of the evening. It was, taken all in all, a pretty ordinary fuck. The next morning we made plans to meet again that night. We even joked about it, you know, about what a super-fucking good time we'd have, and if you ask me, we could've probably really gotten into something incredible if we'd tried again, but when I went to the hospital I found out good old Mom had croaked sometime during the night and somehow, I still don't know why to this day . . . I never got in touch with Susan again. And vice versa. It's a funny thing, you know. At the funeral there were all these people. Friends of Mom's— I didn't know any of them. They were all crying like crazy and I . . . well . . . (*Pause.*) I never even got to the burial. The car I was in broke down on the Merritt Parkway. Just as well. I didn't feel like seeing all those people. I'd sure love to have fucked Susan again, though.

*   *   *

(*Abstract.*) Anyway . . . I just didn't feel like telling anyone. I mean, I wasn't all that upset. I was a little upset, mostly because I thought I ought to be more upset, but as for your actual grief, well. Anything interesting happen to you this semester . . . Kathy? (KATHY *has risen.*) Going? (KATHY *is going out the door.*) Give my regards to that guy you're rescuing at the moment, what's-his-name. (KATHY *is gone.* BOB *shrugs. The cat wanders in from the hallway.*) Hey, cat, what are you doing hanging around here? All the humans gone west. (*Puts the cat outside and shuts the door. He nudges the tiles with his toe and looks around at the empty room.*) Hey, guys, guess what happened to me. I want to tell you about this really incredible thing that happened to me . . . (*He is faltering now, choking slightly but he doesn't know he's about to crack. His body is doing something strange, unfamiliar.*) Hey, what's happening . . . (*He's crying now.*) Oh fuck, come on, come on. Shit, no, no . . .

A RAISIN IN THE SUN

Lorraine Hansberry

This monologue is Asagai's, the young African student, explaining himself to Beneatha, a black American girl. One interjection by her is deleted and marked by asterisks. For more background on this play, see page 33.

◆—◆—◆

ASAGAI.

(*Shouting over her*) *I live the answer!* (*Pause*) In my village at home it is the exceptional man who can even read a newspaper . . . or who ever *sees* a book at all. I will go home and much of what I will have to say will seem strange to the people of my village . . . But I will teach and work and things will happen, slowly and swiftly. At times it will seem that nothing changes at all . . . and then again . . . the sudden dramatic events which make history leap into the future. And then quiet again. Retrogression even. Guns, murder, revolution. And I even will have moments when I wonder if the quiet was not better than all that death and hatred. But I will look about my village at the illiteracy and disease and ignorance and I will not wonder long. And perhaps . . . perhaps I will be a great man . . . I mean perhaps I will hold on to the substance of truth and find my ways always with the right course . . . and perhaps for it I will be butchered in my bed some night by the servants of empire . . .

*   *   *

. . . or perhaps I shall live to be a very old man respected and esteemed in my new nation . . . And perhaps I shall hold office and this is what I'm trying to tell you, Alaiyo; perhaps the things I believe now for my country will be wrong and outmoded, and I will not understand and do terrible things to have things my way or merely to keep my power. Don't you see that there will be young men and women, not British soldiers then, but my own black countrymen . . . to step out of the shadows some evening and slit my then useless throat? Don't you see they have always been there . . . that they always will be. And that such a thing as my own death will be an advance? They who might kill me even . . . actually replenish me!

HOME FREE!

Lanford Wilson

This one-act play opens with a long monologue delivered by Lawrence. He is described as dark, attractive, and about twenty-five years old. At the opening of the play, he is tapping the wall with the end of a coat hanger to get the attention of his "audience," Claypone and Edna, his students for the moment. The scene brings together Lawrence and his girlfriend, Joanna. The dialogue between the two moves at a dizzying speed, vacillating between bizarre, humorous fantasy and the real problem of a baby on the way.

•◆•

LAWRENCE.
Now, if you'll only pay attention! The Pleiades are called the Seven Sisters because they're grouped closely together and with the unaided eye you can only see seven of them. Actually they're about thirty stars in the whole cluster. Now you know that the universe is expanding; we discussed that—Billy, sit down and don't chew your eraser—we discussed that last time. I know your name isn't Billy, Claypone, but you're pretending to be Billy: can't you just sit still like a good student? You're in Astronomy

181

101. If Edna can sit quietly, so can you. Now. As the universe is expanding and all of our galaxy is rotating, within the galaxy the stars are moving at incredible speeds in various directions. It's part of the expansion—Edna!—theory that all stars are moving farther and farther from each other. But the Seven Sisters, although they seem to be perfectly stationary to us, it has been proved that they are shooting away from the center—moving apart, at an incredible speed— every one getting farther from the others, so in a million years we won't be able to tell that they ever were a part of the same cluster. They're shooting out this way! [*Drawing, as with chalk, on the wall.*] And over here, and zoom—at about a hundred light-years a minute! Up and down and out and across—[*Getting uncontrollably excited, he starts tracing their path around the room as if following an exploded skyrocket.*]—and bang! And pow! And, if we was there, Whizz! Burn! Zing! Sssssstt Sssssstt! Zooommmm! Kachowwie! Whamm! [*He has knocked some papers off the desk. He turns to Claypone, calming down.*] Hey, did I scare you? Did I? Where's Edna? [*His eyes focus under the desk across the room. Panting.*] You— come on back here, now. Come on. Sit down. You too, Claypone. It's part of the lesson. I'm busy now. You do something. I don't care; do anything. Don't bother me. [*He walks to the Ferris wheel, sitting, looking at it; turning it gently. To himself.*] No, no, if it went faster you wouldn't need the seats, because the gravity would throw you against the bars; either that or it would throw you off altogether. Well, that way is all right, too; it's just that it's a different ride altogether. You'll have to experiment and see which principle applies to this particular size model. Well it

might mean the death of a hundred-thirty-seven human guinea pigs, but if it's for the advancement of entertainment, what's a sacrifice? I am an engineer, a scientist, I can only make the models; you can either use them or disregard my advancements. [*To Claypone and Edna.*] No, she went to the grocery—she'll be back in a minute. No, you can't go out and look for her. They'd grab you and lock you in jail in a minute. Because you don't watch for street lights. You do not— every time—[*He is getting nervous, frightened.*]— you go out, you get almost hit with some car or truck and it just drives me crazy trying to keep track of you. And besides you hate it out there. You know how you are! You make me so ashamed—stuttering! And not talking to a person and wilting into some corner like a shade plant. No. She'll be back! She went to the grocery to get a few things! [*Almost uncontrolled.*] And she said she'll be back and she will. You must stay here. No, you stay too. You're not going to leave me here alone; you'd wilt into some corner and they'd come and take you off. [*He forces himself down between the desk and bed, on the floor.*] She'll be right back. She promised. And we'll look in the Surprise Box. She promised. You promised. She just went out for a minute; and she'll be back like always and tell us about the adventure, now. [*Pause. Music. Sweetly now.*] You just sit now, like you were at a social tea with ice cream and cake and peppermint frosting and little sugar cookies with butter and almond flavoring. And little sugar crystals on top that are red and blue and yellow and white. . . . [*There is a soft but very urgent knock at the door.*] Shhhhhhh! [*Violently whispered to Claypone and Edna.*] Be quiet! [*The knock is repeated a little louder.*] Shhh!

BALM IN GILEAD

Lanford Wilson

The following monologue takes place in an all-night coffee shop and on the street corner outside, where lost souls seem to congregate. The character, Dopey, is described as one of the "hoods" and is actually a hustler-addict. He has been standing on the corner and now turns and talks directly to the audience in the style of the play.

●◆●

DOPEY.
What he's saying—about renting rooms and all—see—well, there's no reason for it but when a girl—or around here anyway most of the girls have a guy that—kinna looks after them. After all, it's a rough neighborhood; but that's not the only way he looks after them, if you follow my meaning. And the girl sorta keeps him. The guys that are lucky. He lives up in the room—sleeps in the day and the girl uses the room at night. Maybe you think they're being exploited—the girls, I mean, because they don't get ahead. Every dime goes to the john—that's the fellow. And he eventually pulls out—runs off with it—after

184

he's stashed it in a savings account somewhere. But these girls aren't getting so much exploited because they need these guys. No one's forcing them. One leaves, then right after they get over it they're out looking for someone else. Only someone *better*. You know? Like Ann is probably half expecting her john—this guy's name's Sam, or Sammy; she's half expecting him to leave. He's been around seven or eight months; that's about par for Ann. [*Pause.*] Well, it's because they want someone around and because after all balling with old men all the time can get to be a drag—of course not all of their scores are old men. They get just as many good-looking guys; young fellows; high school kids and like that, they pay. Well, maybe you don't like to hear that but they do. So it's not that they get sick of the old men all the time. But these guys that they ball, they aren't—around. You know? They aren't *around*. They want probably to know someone probably. See they're—well. And they don't get new things! I mean these girls don't go out and get themselves dresses and jewelry and things. I mean they get things, but not for themselves, see; for the guy who's with them. New clothes and rings and stuff—all kinds of crap and well because it's no kind of a lark crawling in and out of bed all night and in the morning they maybe want someone who won't leave, see. Won't get up and take off. [*Very quick.*] And then they buy these guys things so the guys around can see how they keep their johns in luxury, you know. [*Pause.*] It's natural as anything. They want someone familiar. You know—to know somebody's touch or their manner or like the texture of his skin. Even if the guy's still asleep in the morning. You can picture it. And this usually keeps them from getting much else. That's what he's trying to tell her only she'll know after a while anyway because it's just a natural thing. So she'll find it out anyway but not till she's there herself.

WHERE HAS
TOMMY FLOWERS GONE?

Terrence McNally

This is a free-flowing play with flexible stage directions by the author, who states that "the places of the play are here, there, and everywhere." The site for the following monologue is on an airplane, which can be suggested by a row of chairs. Tommy is sitting with an empty seat next to him, and he is holding a glass of champagne. He has just made a list of the people who have helped make him what he is, and it is clear that Tommy is a product of the 1960s. The following monologue is close to the beginning of the play, when he notices the pretty airline attendant.

•◆•

TOMMY.

May I have a little more champagne, mon petit lapin? Her name's Greta Prince and I'm crazy about her legs. I've had my eye on her since they called the flight. So far I'm batting zero but I've still got about another hour and a half. You see, I don't know where I'm going to sleep when I get back to the Big Apple tonight. I thought I was on my way home today but I decided not to go after all. Home means St. Petersburg, Florida. It's famous for green benches, orange Rexall drug-stores, pale old people and death. I love it. I just wanted to make sure everyone back home was all right, you know? I mean I didn't particularly want to talk to anyone, just see them again. Well, maybe next time. (*Tommy is looking out the win-dow.*) You know what America looks like at one in the morning from 33,000 feet? A big dark place with a couple of tiny twinkling lights. It's so empty down there! (*The seat begins to revolve and the airplane lights fade down.*) No doubt about it, flying gets you very philosophical. So does look-ing at America from 33,000 feet. At ground level you just get either very scared or very depressed. (*Change of light cue. Tommy appears over the top of the airplane seat. He has on a red baseball cap worn backwards and a scarf. He starts skimming stones.*)

In the first place, it was a dumb question. "Who are the ten most admired men in America today and why?" That's almost as dumb as when they ask you what you want to be when you grow up. And so I wrote your name ten times. Holden Caulfield. Holden Caulfield. Holden Caulfield. Holden Caulfield. Holden Caulfield. Holden Caulfield, Holden Caulfield, Holden Cauffield. Holden Caulfield. Holden Caulfield. "Because he's not a phony" and I got an F. (*To us, as he stops skimming stones.*) I always knew it would happen like this. I'd just be walking along the beach one night, skimming stones, and I'd see this kid just my age, looking just like me, and wearing the same red baseball cap and he'd just be walking and skimming, too, and when we final-ly got close together we'd both stop walking and start skimming together and without really saying anything—anything phony like "What school do you go to?"—we'd just kind of drift into this really natural conversation. (*Tommy starts skimming stones again.*) And then my parents had to go talk to Mr. Bartlett, our principal, and they all decided they didn't know what to do with me and then I had to go see Mr. Bartlett with them and they told me there was no way anyone anywhere could answer Holden Caulfield is even *one* of then most admired men in America today on his civics test and get away with it and how Miss Pearce had practically had a hemorrhage when she read my paper because she had such high hopes for me this semester and I would have to apologize to her and who the hell was Holden Caulfield anyway? and no wonder I was smoking in the boys' lavatory between classes and if I kept it up my growth would be stunted and I was short enough for my age as it was and hadn't my parents promised me a convertible if I didn't smoke until I graduated from high school? which is such a phony offer I almost puked because who wants a convertible *after* they graduate from high school, I'll probably be married by then or in the army or college maybe, and all the time we're in Bartlett's office he's scratching his balls, right in front of everyone, I was getting sick to my stomach, and my father is trying to sound stern and my mother is shaking her head, and all I'm thinking is how much I'd like to get out of there and have a Lucky Strike and maybe go over to Jan Moody's and hack around if her parents were still out of town—she is probably the most developed girl for her age in this state, 38D, I heard. You know, cup size. Sound good to you?—when Bartlett, still scratching his balls, and my mother's right in front of him, I should've called his bluff, "Stop scratching your balls, Bartlett!" when Bartlett asks if I want to take the test again and answer it properly this time and I looked at the three of them very calmly and said "okay" and went into another room and wrote "The ten most admired men in America today are Eisenhower, Truman, Acheson, etc., etc., etc., *because* etc., etc., etc." and I came back and handed it to them and Bartlett read it and smiled at my parents and then he smiled at me and said "You see, that wasn't so hard, was it now?" and I said "No, sir. It was very easy and now *I'm* a phony" and Bartlett was so shook up he even forgot to scratch his balls and said something about expelling me and they all agreed they'd talk about it later and we drove home with nobody saying a word and when we got there the phone was ringing and it was my big brother calling from California before he got shipped off to Korea and I couldn't think of much to say to him and so I said "Just don't get killed over there," which is just about the best and least phony thing I can think of to say to someone who's going off to Korea, especially your brother, and that started a new outburst from my mother and so I walked out of the house and went over to Jan Moody's, only her parents were back, but I tried to peek in her window anyway, she likes to sit around *nude* practically, and all I did was get my shoes muddy and ruin some of her mother's goddamn prizewinning roses and so I came down here and I'm very glad to have this opportunity to offer you a Lucky Strike, tell you I really do consider you the most admired man in America today because you're not a phony and ask you about Times Square. When I finally get to New York City I'm going to stand there for the entire first week just looking at people. You know what they call it? The Crossroads of the World. That's right where I want to be. There's nothing to look at in this town except Jan Moody's knockers. Maybe we could go together. I mean you know about subways and things. (*Pause.*) Seventh Avenue and 42nd St. I was there. Holden wasn't. (*Lights come up in airplane. The seat revolves and we see Tommy looking out the plane window as Greta returns with champagne.*) Did you dig Marilyn Monroe?

WHERE HAS TOMMY FLOWERS GONE?

Terrence McNally

Though he has tried to be friendly, Tommy has just been told by a police officer to move on. This is the last scene in the play. For more about it, see page 187.

• ◆ •

TOMMY.

I'm moving. Don't worry. I'm moving. Every-body's moving. I've got a date with Elizabeth Taylor. We're going to an after hours club in Port Aransas, Texas. We'll shoot craps in the back room and drink tequila like the Mexicans: straight, with a piece of lime and a little salt. She'll like that, Liz. And there's a girl I know in San Francisco I'm gonna see again. She'll drive us to Tiburon in her Mustang and we'll sit on the dock eating abalones. Sure we will. And then I'm going to play touch football on the beach at Hyannisport with the surviving Kennedys and we'll all go out in sailboats singing songs of the day. Sound good to you, officer? You are so fucking handsome when you smile like that. Excuse me for saying this but just talking to you

I feel like some fucking handsome ten foot tall prince myself. And if anybody wants me now they're never gonna find me because I'm never gonna stay. Tell them. I had green stripes, a dog named Arnold, and I walked in backwards until they thought I was coming out. Tell them my name was Tommy Flowers. Tell them I was a prince. (*To us.*) Bet he can't count to ten without smiling. (*He goes.*)

WHERE HAS TOMMY FLOWERS GONE?

Terrence McNally

◆

This humorous monologue is delivered by an English sheepdog. The author suggests an actor in a dog suit. But he saw and was satisfied with an actor on his hands and knees and playing the part in a long gray turtleneck sweater.

ARNOLD.

I didn't always have Tommy Flowers and I'm not at all sure I always will. I got him when I was given back to him by a friend of his who didn't want me after Tommy had given me to him in the first place. It's complicated, I know. This friend was a very lonely sort of person and Tommy decided that he should have a dog. Only he didn't want a dog. But when he saw me something inside of him must have snapped because his eyes kind of filled up like he was going to cry and he held me very close. I was this big then! And he didn't say anything and he walked a few feet away from everyone and stood with his back to them and just held me like a little baby. No one had to ask if he wanted me. You could just tell. I was so happy. But the next morning he didn't want me at all. There I was, just kind of slumped in my box, all droopy-eyed and warm-nosed and not looking at all too hot. Puppy chill is all it was. Tommy said they'd just take me to the vet but the friend didn't want a sick dog. He didn't want any dog. And you know what his reason was? They die on you. That's what he said. They die on you. We do, you know. Everything does. But is that a reason? How could anyone not want me? Oh, don't get any ideas. I'm not a talking dog. I'm a thinking one. There's a difference! (*Lights out on Arnold.*)

HELLO OUT THERE

William Saroyan

This is a one-act play that takes place in a little jail house in Matador, Texas. A young man has been arrested for rape. Although he is innocent, he is also a drifter and gambler and is unknown in the area. He is alone in the jail except for a young girl, plain and shy, who cleans up at night. In his fear and loneliness, he talks to the girl through the bars. The girl's short lines are deleted in the following scene and marked with asterisks.

• ◆ •

YOUNG MAN.

You just pack up and wait for me. We'll high-roll the hell out of here to San Francisco.

*   *   *

I been lonesome all my life—there's no cure for that—but you and me—we can have a lot of fun hanging around together. You'll bring me luck. I know you will.

*   *   *

I'm a gambler. I don't work. I've *got* to have
luck or I'm no good. I haven't had any luck
in years. Two whole years now—one place to
another. Bad luck all the time. That's why I got
in trouble back there in Wheeling, too. That was
no accident. That was my bad luck following me
around. So here I am, with my head half busted.
I guess it was her old man that did it.

*   *   *

No, her husband. If I had an old lady like that,
I'd throw her out.

*   *   *

It's no good searching the streets for anything
that might be there at the time. You got to have
somebody with you all the time. You got to have
somebody who's right. Somebody who knows
you, from way back. You got to have somebody
who even knows you're wrong but likes you just
the same. I know I'm wrong, but I can't help it. If
you go along with me, I'll be the best man anybody ever saw. I won't be wrong any more. You
know when you get enough money, you *can't* be
wrong any more—you're right because the money says so. I'll have a lot of money and you'll be
just about the prettiest girl in the whole world.
I'll be proud walking around San Francisco with
you on my arm and people turning to look at
us.

*   *   *

When I get back in some decent clothes, and you're on my arm—well, Katey, they'll turn and look, and they'll see something, too.

*   *   *

Yeah—that's your name from now on. You're the first girl I ever called Katey. I've been saving it for you. O.K.?